The BPD Journals II:

Remission and Relapse

Topher Edwards

March 2014 – January 2016

Once again, I dedicate this book to my family. Though you do not know about these books yet, I hope someday you can appreciate why I am writing them.

This book is also dedicated to my amazing girlfriend M. Your support and encouragement mean more to me than you may ever know. All my love.

"Depression is a disorder of mood, so mysteriously painful and elusive in the way it becomes known to the self—to the mediating intellect—as to verge close to being beyond description."

-William Styron

Preface

I have decided to continue chronicling my life. A lot has changed in the years since my last series of journals, and my hope is that readers will see that there can be a light at the end of the tunnel. Mental illness is not always a death sentence, but sadly for some, it can be. It has been a long, treacherous, twisty road full of obstacles and setbacks, but I can say that I am still here. For the malady from which I suffer, there is no cure – only treatment. The upside is that the treatment I have received turned out to be quite effective. Although I cannot say that life is a cakewalk now and all of my troubles are behind me, I can say that I am better equipped to deal with the often horrific symptoms characteristic of my disease. As a refresher from my last collection, my official diagnosis is borderline personality disorder, with major depressive disorder and generalized anxiety disorder to top it off. This trifecta of illness has truly tested the limits of my psyche and of my body.

Every day I am reminded of my dreadful past by the scars that line my arms. A select few call them "battle scars"; a sign that I fought an illness and overcame it. A larger majority see it in a much more negative light. I admit there is a certain amount of shame, and I make every effort to cover them up. I would like to not care what people think of me, but that is not so easy. Despite all the efforts at reducing the stigma associated with mental illness, we still have a LONG way to go. Some wear their scars as a badge of honour, but for me it is a permanent reminder that on more than one occasion I wanted to end my life. It is a reminder that I had no respect for my body and that my obsession with self-destruction nearly killed me.

It is often hard to articulate exactly what is on my mind, to define something as obscure and subjective as depression. It is a disease that takes on many forms with varying degrees of severity. To each person it is different, with different manifestations, durations, and outcomes. This is why it is so hard to treat and often many different therapies are used, and it is not uncommon for two or more therapies to be used concurrently. Of course, for me, depression is only one side of the die – borderline personality disorder in itself is very unpredictable, with a rather frightening prognosis. Anywhere from 70 – 80% of those diagnosed with BPD attempt suicide and/or engage in self-injurious behaviour. About 10% of those with BPD will successfully commit suicide. As of now, it is a very misunderstood disorder, but much progress is being made to understand and find effective treatment for it.

Now, back to the main purpose here. I must forewarn – despite coming a long way from cutting and filling my body with drugs, these posts you are about to read are not always positive. There seems to (still) exist an inner turmoil; a chaos between my id and super-ego that is never-ending. From time to time, Darkness prevails, whether I like it or not. What I have learned is that the measure of who I am is not whether darkness exists in me (as it does in everyone), the true measure is whether or not I let it win.

Therein lies the purpose of this volume – to show that even though darkness exists in everyone, it does not always win. I used to let it win. I thrived on the chaos that was created when I did, and did not care about the consequences. Though sometimes there is a temptation to revert back to old ways, I have come too far to fall. Too much is at stake, and I have too many people who care about me and want to see me live well.

Note that the first few entries were posted to an online journal, long before I began compiling these entries into volumes. Once I began my first book, I realized it was much easier to skip the online posts.

Enjoy!

- XV

Initium Novum
March 17th, 2014

I reopened this journal, purging all the previous entries. They were crap. Weak. What I need now is a way to clear my head. In the last year I went from a druggie that used every day, no job, no ambitions. What am I now? I'm in school, heading into the Paramedic program... But what has really changed?

Am I really so different than who I was a year ago? I still feel weak. I still run to substance to fill the massive void I feel.

So is this truly a new beginning?

It is very hard for me to rid myself of the pessimism. If history has shown anything, it is that once things start to look good, a little too good, there is always a shit storm that comes and destroys all that I have built.

The truth is that I do not feel stable. Despite my medications, despite being in school, the old demons still call my name... louder lately than usual. So what do I do?

I can't go back to how I was before... I just can't. No matter what it takes...

- XV

Pieces
March 20th, 2014

I feel like I am unravelling. Slowly, as if single threads are being plucked from me. It's the old familiar darkness creeping back in. I don't know why this is happening to me, but I know where this road leads. I've walked it before, in a haze of drugs, covered in my own blood.

Let's not go there.

- XV

Well ... That Was Unexpected
March 21st, 2014

It's refreshing to know that despite my extensive background in drugs, that sometimes there is a slight variation... or a cut... that lends a whole new experience. Holy shit.

I can hear him calling... Crawling... I have to be stronger.

- XV

Sileo
July 12th, 2014

I've decided to come back to writing. It has been a few months (less than I remember). A lot has changed, and a lot has not. I am no longer going to be a paramedic, but get my Bachelor of Science degree instead. With that fun little update out of the way, let us continue with the true intention of this journal - to let the darkness out, without shame or apologies.

Life is funny, in a sick and twisted way. It can lead you on, make you feel at ease, and raise your morale. Here is the twist: Hiding beneath is a large, steaming vat of shit ready to be dumped at any time. Inside us all is a darkness, just as there is a light. Which we show is equal parts who we are and the decisions we make.

Wording this post is a tedious and laborious task. Do I really want to beat around the bush, worrying that I will be identified and faced with consequences? That is a sad reality of our world. The dark part of ourselves is the elephant in the room that everyone side-steps, ignores, and gives you the stink-eye if you point it out.

Frankly, I am tired of beating around the bush. Fuck that noise, I am done. If you cannot face or handle the big dark elephant, close your browser now and go play outside. Otherwise, cuddle up with your favourite alcoholic beverage and read on.

- XV

Novi Saeculi
March 21st

If I am anything, I am inconsistent. Once again I have left and come back to writing. The reason? Fuck if I know... But between this and my written "works", maybe I can put some order into this chaos that I still feel. For the most part, life has been exponentially more bearable than before. That is not to say that it has been easy, by any means. Here now is a brief synopsis of the last six months:

- Started my Bachelor of Science in Nursing program
- Met an amazing girl, whom I now call my own
- Got booted from said Bachelor's program for having a criminal record
- Starting a Bachelor's Psychology program

I did say brief, yeah? Life has been "funny" of late, and it seems to be the constant struggle between "good" and "bad", a dichotomy that I have always had close a hand throughout the last decade of my life.

For example, despite the fact that I excelled in my Bachelor of Science program, I was still forced to leave because of a five year old charge from a mentally unstable ex. Saying she was unstable is my way of trying to be the bigger person in this whole situation. Even five years later, she finds a way to cut me down. If it wasn't for the aforementioned amazing girl, my family, few close friends, and years of learning to deal with pain, this school thing would have sent me into a downward spiral. It would have been a messy, drug-addled fuster-cluck. Don't get me wrong, I could have dealt with it better, and there were a few drugs, but for the most part I (for the first time) saw just how far I had come in the last few years.

I grew, from an emotionally unstable (another understatement) druggie into what I believe to be a relatively stable individual who now only dabbles in the odd drug. Despite this growth, there is still something inside me, something insidious. Borderline personality disorder is something that they say some people recover from, but I feel like there is simply too much damage, too many memories, too many scars to ever fully recover. I can't forget the Hell I went through, the Hell I put others through. All I can do now is adapt to a life where things don't suck as much, where I have support and more love for myself than I had before.

I understand this will be a life-long mission of fighting the Demons that try to claw their way to the surface, but at least I have the means to hold them back. Sometimes though I can feel their claws more than others. Sometimes it is harder to push them back down than others, and it shows.

All in all, progress has been made, and progress is still in... progress... and I feel a hope that I have not felt in a long time. I don't know the true purpose of reopening this journal, but maybe it will occur to me one day. Maybe it will help me sort some shit out and figure out what my path truly is. For now, it is just to kill time and empty some of the thought-noise out of my head.

- XV

A Trip Down Memory Lane
March 22nd

As I re-opened this account, I happened to come across an old one that I had forgotten about. Over 200 posts spanning one year. It was shocking, to say the least, what I had written during that time. So what did I do? I spent hours copying each and every entry into a Word document, in order, no edits, no omissions. Why? I have no fucking clue. Maybe I'm just spontaneous like that. I haven't even read them all yet, but the ones I did read are quite... disturbing (to say the least).

Maybe one day I will find use for them, or maybe it was just a way to kill a few hours. Maybe it is dangerous to look into a past so riddled with blood, drugs, depression, and depravity. Frankly, I am amazed that I survived at all. But I truly feel like I am stronger today because of what I went through (as cliché as that sounds). I have overcame a lot over the last several years, and I am proud of that.

For the first time in a while, I have a relatively clear idea of what I want to do with my life. I also have an amazing girlfriend and the best family and friends. I feel like this journal will be exponentially more positive than the one I mentioned above.

-XV

Just Remission?
March 23rd

Lately I have been feeling down. I have a lot in my life to be happy about, and I am aware of that. Yet sometimes I feel the old familiar feelings of depression and hate that once plagued me. Sleep is still a huge problem too. I really, really, REALLY do not want to fall back into old habits and old ways, but sometimes it feels inevitable. The BPD, the depression, and the anxiety are by no means cured, and seem to be creeping closer to the surface than they have for a while. Being forced to leave school, again, took its toll. I just can't seem to be truly happy. There is always the voice that tells me I am not okay, and I don't know whether or not I should listen to it or ignore it. A decision must be made if this continues. I cannot afford to let it worsen to the point where I fall back to where I was before. I just can't.

- XV

Veritas
March 24th

The truth is, I don't know what is going on. I seem to be on the razor's edge, teetering on the edge of falling back into old feelings and ways. I hope that I am wrong, I really do. I just can't ignore the way I feel. She says to let go of the past, to forgive myself. How? She says to face what is going on. How? I know that inside me there is still the person who is capable of terrible things, the Darkness that threatens to surface. Sure, I am a lot better at pushing the Demons back down than I was before, but how long can this really last? Do I have what it takes to keep the momentum going towards health and a happier future, or will I fall back down as far as I have climbed? The higher I go, the further the fall. Potential energy stored, waiting for the relentless pull of gravity to convert it into kinetic energy. What goes up must come down, they say. Hopefully I am an exception. I have lived too many days in misery; hating myself, my life, and my circumstance. I used to be helpless and weak. I can't go back. I won't.

- XV

Old Feelings
March 25th

I woke up today feeling anxious. It quickly became worse, with shaking, sweaty palms, and a racing heart. I had a feeling of dread that I had not felt in a while. Please don't let this be further proof I am slipping back into how I was before. I thought I was done with that shit but it seems to be coming back. I will not get ahead of myself, but I cannot ignore something like this, something I haven't felt in almost a year... Shit.

- XV

Infirmus
March 26th

More evidence to the decline. I don't feel right. My mood is shit, my sleep is shittier, my appetite is low, and my anxiety is bad. It's beginning to feel like the olden days of depression and misery. My hopes that this is just a phase are dwindling, though it hasn't been long enough for me to be sure this is my illness coming back, I can't help but worry. The old familiar weight is on me and I can already feel the effects.

I made an appointment with a councillor I used to see years ago who now works at the College for next Tuesday. I hope she can figure things out and put everything into perspective for me. I also called my doctor to make an appointment and am waiting to hear back. On Monday I see a plastic surgeon to find out what he can do about the scars on my arms. I'm hoping the consult brings good news. I am tired of covering up my shame. The scars (to others) show a person who is sick and "crazy". For me, they are a constant reminder of my ugly, sordid past that I want removed. Getting rid of the scars on the outside certainly won't heal those on the inside, but it's a step toward leading a life where I don't have to make excuses or cover them up.

I hate that I am this way. Though the journals I have kept over the years sometimes show a man who has accepted, and even embraced, his illness, that is far from the truth. I want to be happy, I want to be okay. I just cannot seem to be. At least not for an extended period of time. Again, here comes the fine line between pessimism and realism.

- XV

Dead End
March 30th

I had high hopes for a consultation with a local plastic surgeon about the scars on my arms. I am sick of wearing long-sleeved shirts, hiding my shame from everyone around me. It's not that I hate them, but I hate how others see them, and me as a result. The way I see it, they are performing amazing surgeries every day. They can take someone's heart out and transplant it into another person's body... and it works! They can even grow a fucking ear on a mouse to transplant onto a human. So why did I walk in that room and get bad news? NOTHING can be done? Seriously?? I guess I put too much faith into someone named Dr. Dickie, but hey, I thought maybe I'd catch a fucking break.

Speaking of catching things, I am also sick. With what, I have no idea, but it came just in time for my birthday (two days ago). I rarely get sick, which is surprising, but when I do, it's bad. I had to leave work today because not only was I sick as fuck, but the medication I am taking for it is making me loopy.

My birthday was alright, She made my day, as I knew she would. It's the little things she does that mean the world to me. Despite me booking a table for 15 and only 5 people showing up (INCLUDING me), it wasn't a bad night. My friend had to call some of his friends just so it didn't look so pathetic. I know I have pushed a lot of people away, and burned a lot of bridges in the process, but I was still surprised to see how few people would come for a simple dinner for my birthday. As I always say, it's just another day. Celebrate my Mom, she did all the work! I guess my Dad did too... Anyway another year has passed and I still seem uncertain of who I am or who I want to be. Maybe THIS will be the year that changes things for me. Maybe not.

I have an appointment with my old counsellor tomorrow who now works at the college. Hopefully I can articulate how I am feeling and she can try to make some sense of it. I need her to tell me that I am not falling back into old feelings, that this is a phase... A Quarter-Life Crisis. That fraction is being far too optimistic for me, however. I have aged myself with my blatant disregard for my own well-being, so realistically, more like a Third-Life Crisis. I will post about the appointment tomorrow... Or maybe not... Does it really matter?

- XV

Zombie Jesus
April 3rd

Easter weekend is upon us, and frankly, I don't give a shit. What do bunnies and chocolate have to do with the supposed resurrection of our lord and saviour?? Nadda.

I think I'm almost over this cold or flu or whatever the hell it is. Over a week and a half of feeling like shit and I am slowly recovering. That is my excuse for not posting on here more, not that it really matters anyway. Some good news, however - Manson just posted a new tour and is coming to Toronto in August with The Smashing Pumpkins!! If I can see him twice in the same year I will be a happy fucking camper. Nothing is going to stop me from going to that show. Should be good!

Not really much to say. My mood has been about the same, and being sick has kind of made that take a back seat. Seeing my old councillor on Tuesday helped me sort some shit out and make sense of what is going on. I am planning on seeing her for next few weeks, and hopefully I can get over this funk I have been in lately.

- XV

What?
April 16th

It's been almost two weeks since my last post. I never said I was consistent. I feel especially shitty today. My girlfriend is going home for the summer on Sunday, and surely that is contributing to my shit mood. I seem to be letting things get to me that normally wouldn't. Little things that I internalize and blow up into something bigger than it actually is. I'm noticing more and more that my life is not what I want it to be. I am moving in the right direction, but that seems to be the theme here; moving towards something, but never getting there. I have always been told that I can do whatever I want; that I have potential. Then why, after all this time, am I still living with my mother (at 25), still switching University programs, still in debt, and still miserable? The dissonance between what I am told and the harsh reality of my life is causing me to question everything.

Seeing my therapist is helping a bit, but I can't seem to verbalize what is going on inside my head. It's chaos, and the noise is keeping me awake at night and irritable during the day. I decided to give my doctor a call and see about going back on antidepressants. With my mood dropping and my girlfriend leaving for the summer, I need to get ahead of this before it gets out of control. I can't go back to how it was before. I've come too far. But at the same time, it feels like I have barely moved an inch. Maybe one day I will figure my life out, but for now, I guess I'll just keep spinning my tires and hope that some clarity comes soon.

- XV

Reversion
April 21st

I went to the doctor today and was re-prescribed Wellbutrin - an antidepressant. I have been off these types of medications for over a year, but as earlier posts show, I seem to be feeling the old familiar depression and hopelessness. I don't feel too shitty about it, but for me it seems like a step backwards. The depression is not nearly as debilitating as it was before, but I can feel it coming - a poisonous fog rolling in with the potential to suffocate everything I have built. This is more to get ahead of a potentially catastrophic situation. With Her gone for the summer, and of course the incurable mental illness, I cannot be too careful when it comes to feelings like this. I guess we will see how this works out, but in conjunction with my counselling, I am hoping this will be enough to prevent my mood from getting any worse.

I am hoping for a lot, preparing for the worst, but taking the steps I think I need to in order to beat this - whatever it is. I will try to keep this journal up to date, for myself (it is private anyways), but I have been known to be quite flaky with posting.

Here we go...

- XV

S.A.F.
April 22nd

I had to leave work early and take the day off tomorrow because, as my post title shows, I am sick as fuck. It's just a cold, but I hate missing work and feeling this way. It's day two of Wellbutrin and I am hoping that the side-effects are mild. I have been on them before and they are one of the few antidepressants that didn't fuck me up too much. Here's to hoping that these work again, and that I can get over these feelings of sadness and hopelessness. As I said before, I have come too far to fail. The higher you climb, the further you have to fall. That must be why I spent so many years near rock bottom.

I miss Her already, even though it's only been a few days. I think it's more because it's going to be four months away from her (with the odd visit). FML this sucks ass. Anyway, She is calling me so... Peace.

- XV

Well Fuck
April 24th

I have a brutal cold that seems to want to hang around for a while. I've been pretty much bed-ridden for the last few days and it shows no sign of letting up. On top of that, I'm sure the Wellbutrin side-effects are starting, or at least will soon. My appetite is already down and sleep is impossible. Of course my doctor won't change my sleeping meds; he'd rather me stick with something that is no longer as effective.

I miss Her. I'm seeing her Sunday for a few hours, then who knows when after that. Four months barely seeing her is going to be hard, and will certainly make these new antidepressants worth taking. I just feel like a dark cloud is approaching; the slight shadow blocking the sun is already visible and I fear the worst. Maybe that's just my nature, to assume that bad things will always happen. If I use history as an indicator, then I'm truly fucked... But positive thoughts must win. I cannot afford to slip again. Too much is at stake and I have come too far. There isn't much else to do but dwell when I am stuck in bed feeling like death, with the early side-effects of the new medication (and all the ones I'm taking for my cold) taking it's toll.

Good things are happening though. I got a full-time job in the Summer, I have a girlfriend that I love with all my heart, and my Dark Passenger seems to be gone (with the exception of some slight whisperings). All I can do is live day by day and hope for the best. Look at me being all optimistic. That's a new one.

- XV

Flashback: 2012
April 25th

I was cleaning my room today (a rare occurrence to begin with) and came across an old SD card hidden in the bottom of my drawer. Upon opening it on my computer, it looked just like regular photography that I used to do... Until it wasn't. An incredibly graphic picture of my arm all cut up, lined with stitches appeared. I gotta say it was disturbing, to say the least. I had forgotten how severe the damage was, and again I am shocked I survived. As if that wasn't enough to make me pop a Clonazepam, later on in the pictures were "artsy" photos of cocaine, syringes, pills, and other drug paraphernalia. The spoon was laid out, filled with cocaine, water, and a cigarette filter. Next to it was the syringe, and a pile of coke. In the background - four prescription bottles of various antidepressants, sedatives, benzos, and anti-psychotics.

Again, I am amazed I didn't die from that too. It's amazing how low I sank, and that was barely three years ago. I have come a long way, but the triggers still exist. I can never be cured of my illness, and the potential for full catharsis is limited. I have learned to accept my diagnosis, and even learned ways to deal with the symptoms as they come. But seeing these long-lost photos was a reminder that the past isn't so distant. That I am still the same person I was then. That the possibility of backsliding into self-destruction is ever present.

I guess I should throw a positive thing into this post, at the request of my therapist. I see Meagan tomorrow. Only for a few hours, but even a few seconds with her is bliss. This is going to be a long summer; a true test of our relationship, as well as my emotional stability. All I can do is try to think happy thoughts and not let His whisperings get to me (as tempting as they sometimes are).

- XV

I'm Not A Birthday Present
April 25th

*"I don't know if I can open up
I've been opened enough
I don't know if I can open up
I'm not a birthday present
I'm aggressive aggressive
The past is over
Now the passive seems so pathetic*

*Are we fated, faithful, or fatal?
Are we fated, faithful, or fatal?*

*I'm feeling stoned and alone like a heretic
And I'm ready to meet my maker
I feel stoned and alone like a heretic
I'm ready to meet my maker
Lazarus got no dirt on me
Lazarus got no dirt on me
And I rise to every occasion
I'm the Mephistopheles of Los Angeles"*

- "The Mephistopheles of Los Angeles" - Marilyn Manson

Twenty-six years and Manson still makes amazing music. His new album is incredible, and as always, his lyrics speak to me.

He has been the constant in my life, through the worst of times and the best. When I tell people he is my idol, I get the look of pure ignorance and judgment that I would love to slap off their smug faces. If they only knew his genius, his insight, his truth. He has been through shit and has the ability to speak to those suffering and tell them that pain is a fact of life, but pain can be overcome... and sometimes embraced.

As for the choice of lyrics, I have opened up and been opened up so many times with negative consequences that I am afraid to anymore. From opening up spilling my heart to a back-stabbing slut to opening my veins in the hopes that it would be enough to kill me; I feel that it only ends in pain and misery. With Her, I do open up, but I hold a lot of things close to the chest, things that I know can only cause harm. She needs to be protected from that part of me, the one that screams for chaos and self-destruction.

She has been absolutely amazing. She understands my history and focuses on how far I have come, not on my past transgressions (excuse the religious vernacular). She is the type of girl I need. But I would be lying if I said I wasn't scared of hurting her too. I have left a trail of mangled bodies with their hearts torn out in my wake, and I don't want her to be yet another victim of who I am. But as I have said before, I am different now. I am not as weak as I used to be and I have a much better chance of being happy, and most of all, making her happy too.

- XV

I'm No Author...
April 27th

I have been toying with the idea of writing a book... Sort of a tell-all about my struggles with mental health, but to focus on the recovery I have made. I've been writing drafts and I can't seem to get out what I want to. No words seem to describe the anguish, the helplessness, the pain, and the emptiness that I felt. Not to mention that all of this is reopening old wounds and making it hard to write. I want to do this so that I can help people - show them that getting better is possible. I want to write my own "Darkness Visible". I want to write something that if I read years ago, it would have made a difference in my life.

But what is better? Lately I haven't been sleeping, barely eating, and this feeling of depression and dread is constant now. I'm scared and I don't know what to do.

- XV

WTF?!
April 27th

I have been reading through my old journals for this book I am apparently writing and... HOLY SHIT! How am I still alive? How am I still (relatively) sane? It was barely four years ago, but it seems like a different person from a different life. It goes to show that no one is beyond repair. No one is too far gone to get help. Sure, I may still have my issues, but they aren't anything like the past. Thank god for that.

- XV

That Old Familiar Feeling
April 28th

I have been working tirelessly on this "book" that I feel I should write. Despite troubles remembering life as it was years ago (clouded by drugs), it is actually going pretty well. It is hard to read my journals and remember just how weak and broken I was, but I am hoping this will all be for the betterment of at least one person's life. I want to write my own "Darkness Visible", a memoir of madness, but with the focus on my recovery. Of course, I will have to spill many gory details of my life at rock-bottom, but the endgame is one of hope. The point is that even at your lowest, there is light ahead. Even a faint glow in the darkness can guide you to a better place.

Ironically, as I write this, I am back on anti-depressants and maybe a few Percocet. But progress is progress, and this will be a lifelong battle against the monster that is mental illness.

- XV

Continuity and Change
May 6th

Some things have changed, some are much the same. Working full-time has been good, and the pay cheques will be even better. I need to get some money in the bank and pay off some debt. Her and I got into one of our first "fights" when she went too far and said I was terrible with money and asked where it was all going. She didn't mean to push it, I guess... But she did cross a line. We resolved the issue pretty quickly. I just don't need reminding that I am in debt from the mistakes of my past, and it is taking me longer to get out of it due to some current "mistakes". She's good with money, and that's great. She also has had five less years to fuck up her credit like I have. I hope she never does. It's yet another remnant of a rough time in my life.

Speaking of which, the scars on my arms are going to be undergoing some laser treatment in a few weeks. The doctor said I should see about 60-70% improvement on the look of them, which is fantastic. Much better than what that shit-knuckle of a plastic surgeon told me before. It's not going to be cheap, but I am sick of covering it up. Long sleeves suck when it's 30 degrees outside. I can only make so many excuses. I never expected my arms to be perfect again, so I am pretty fucking happy with 60-70%.

The Wellbutrin is not doing as much as I thought it would, but I have yet to raise the dose. That will happen the same day I get my arms done. Maybe I'll see more improvement once I'm taking more. It sucks with Her being away for the summer. I miss the fuck out of her, and I'm sure that's not helping things either.

I also found a guy who has Oxy... my old friend. It's been pretty fucking great popping those and going to work, or sitting in the sun having some beers on the weekend. All in all, life is pretty good. It's a work in progress.

- XV

Id
May 8th

You're fucking pathetic. You piss and moan over choices YOU make. Over decisions YOU make. Isn't that what free will is all about? The ability to do as you please, to explore the darker aspects of your being. To stick your toe in the waters of depravity, testing the temperature before you dive in. The time has passed for you to save your "soul". You are gone already. You dug your grave but you are too fucking stubborn to lay down in it and die. You know every pill you pop, every beer you drink, every cigarette you light is bringing you closer to the inevitable. But you fucking do it anyway. How was tonight so different? You wanted something, and you took it. Kudos, motherfucker. Kudos. Stop being such a little bitch about everything and own up to your actions. It's YOU that made them. It's YOU that has to suffer. All I do is tell you what you already know... You want a life where you feel no pain, where, substance is your escape, where depravity is your grace. You have passed the point of no return, so what's one more fuck-up in a loooooong history of fuck-ups? It's a drop in the fucking ocean. So keep chasing your highs, your pleasures, your desires, and stop looking to others to tell you what is right. Stop letting imaginary lines and hypocritical rules dictate your behaviour. You lose in the long run. Face it. You are who you are. Stop trying to change and embrace who you are. I know what you truly want. I know what you desire. I will give you the power to do it, so stop making fucking excuses and feeling sorry for yourself. I'm sick of your bullshit. Man up. Nut up or shut up. This is life. It fucking sucks. Might as well make the most of it, no?

- Id

Moral Compass
May 11th

My moral compass is broken. Permanently stuck at depravity. No matter how hard I try to fake it, or even truly attempt escape, inevitably, I fall back to old ways. There is a long history here of which many are unaware. Of which many would recoil in repulsion and gasp in fear. Smite the Devil who smiles, but we all know. Tear down human nature and build a wall of invisible 'rights' and 'wrongs'. Surround ourselves with happy thoughts and positive morals. That will keep out the demons, no?

NO.

It will not. I've walked the line between life and death, right and wrong, moral and immoral, sober and high; but where have I ended up? I'm still confused. I'm still broken, trying to pick up the pieces of a life I shattered long ago. Trying to get some semblance of normalcy back into my life. But like Sisyphus the King, I am damned to push an immense boulder up a hill, only to watch helplessly as it rolls back down. Sometimes the boulder crushes me, sometimes I have enough strength to dodge it. I've fought so much for so long, but my mask of sanity is slipping. Maybe this all seems overdramatic. Maybe it is the pathetic ramblings of someone with serious issues. Maybe. But maybe I have a point. Maybe I am not wrong about how I feel or the urges that pull me deeper into the void.

Duality of life is a fact. Light versus dark is the theme of my life; the archetype of my being. There must be a reason wrong feels right, and right feels tedious. Freud had a point when he theorized that we are driven by often unconscious, sexual

22

desires. It felt right, so why is it wrong? Because someone said so. Some faceless dictator who decided that what I did is terrible. Or some invisible, absentee deity who proclaimed it a sin. Either way I don't agree, and why should I live my life by rules I don't agree with? The consequences would be disastrous if she found out, and of course I care. I tell her I love her, but words are wind. Maybe my actions speak louder, as the saying goes.

There are an awful lot of maybes leading to a severe lack of resolution. I wish I had the answer, the one brilliant idea that could fix everything, including me. But I don't. All I have are 'maybes' and uncertainties. That is the cross I bear, the psychopathy of my condition. I can't use my diagnosis as a crutch, but I can say it is a factor in how I am. BPD is an unpredictable syndrome characterized by chaos, impulsivity, and instability. I decided to accept my disorder long ago, yet there still lies the question of morality. Do I care? Maybe. Maybe not.

- XV

Tomorrow
May 14th

I see her tomorrow!! Finally, after a LONG ass month. I can't wait. Sleep won't be easy tonight. The distance has been tough, but I think it has been a test. Mistakes were made, and we fought for the first time(s), but we are still together. I would much rather have her here with me all the time, but I'd also much rather the distance than not having her at all. I realize that now, and I'm glad I didn't fuck everything up with rash decisions and other BPD-related bullshit. She is worth it. I love her. That is all that matters in the grand scheme of things. There are still tough months ahead, but we will endure.

Look at me being all optimistic. It's not all roses. I still feel like I am slipping into a state that is all to familiar, that I thought I left in the past. Clearly life has taken its toll and I have not been cured, and never will be. The anti-depressants may be working... But how can I really tell when I'm high on oxy all the time? People around me say I seem happier, but I think it's more the oxy than the Wellbutrin.

Thoughts aren't coming easy right now... Maybe later.

- XV

Burn
May 27th

Yesterday I went to get the scars on my arms treated. It's a new technology called profractional laser (or something like that). They shoot a high powered laser into the scar tissue like a tattoo needle and break it up, causing new collagen to grow. The doctor was optimistic, saying there should be about a 60-70% improvement after two treatments (totalling $1000). They put a numbing cream on, which did fuck all. It was pretty painful and the smell of burning flesh was disgusting. Already it has healed quite a bit, but I am hoping I didn't just flush money down the toilet. They only did one arm because I didn't want to be completely disabled. I go back in three weeks to get the other one done, assuming I am happy with how the first one turned out.

Other than that it has been business as usual for the most part. I still feel shitty a lot of the time, but my antidepressant was just doubled. Hopefully I will see some more improvement in the next month or so. I am in one of my inexplicable shitty moods now, causing me to end the phone conversation with Meagan before I brought her down too. Maybe another day I will have more to talk about.

- XV

I Am Among No One
May 29th

I may be drunk, but I will still try to be articulate as usual. Tonight was rough... A handful of Percocet and a case of beer has numbed me to the point where I am okay with being alone right now. My brother has to work early, my girlfriend is hours away, my friends are busy, and I am alone. However a certain friend surprised me by coming over for a bit to visit! I was pleasantly surprised, but he left after just over an hour. Now I sit here, watching the Blue Jays make a comeback against Minnesota, drunk and high.
I am a mess, and I know it. If she knew I did perks she wouldn't be too happy. But the Dark part of me doesn't care. Does that make me a horrible person? Probably. But that is an existential crisis best left for sobriety. As for my big fuck up, I can't help but fantasize about it... about it happening again, and again, and again. That feeling that is so horribly wrong it becomes right. That lust that pulls me into the void. I want it. I want her too.

What do I do?

Endure.

- XV

The Poisonous Cloud
May 30th

As author William Styron so perfectly described, depression is
like a poisonous cloud rolling in. There is often no reason, no
singular event that brings it on. It is an elusive, indescribable
condition that consumes you. It eats away at your insides until
you become as poisonous as that cloud. You poison yourself,
those you love; anyone around you. At first it is a mysterious
and shocking thing, but once you live with it and endure for
years, it becomes part of you. In fact, after a while, you begin to
embrace it. The dark thoughts you once cringed at are now
relatively 'normal' in your day to day life. Sick depravity, though
repulsive at first, can become your escape. We must all realize
that there is good and evil in everyone - the inescapable
dichotomy that defines us as human beings. No one is all good,
and no one is all bad. In life, we fight to push the darkness down,
pretend it doesn't exist, and focus on the light. It is tiresome
work. Sometimes I wish I could stop fighting the dark (and
sometimes I do). I wish I could release it all and leave my mark
on the world. No, this is not a threat, nor is it a cry for help.

I am pissed
I am poisoned
I am abnormal

I am mentally ill
I am an addict
I am broken
I am.... beyond repair?

I am tired of living by social norms, afraid of the consequences of going against them. It's bullshit. I am done. Fuck it.

- XV

Down
May 31st

It seems no matter what I do, I cannot escape the darkness. Even when life seems good - an amazing girlfriend, school ahead of me, a good job... There is still something deep inside of me that is rotting away. I can wear my masks that I have crafted with care, but the truth is I am miserable. Everyone says I seem better, that I have come so far. Have I? Why do I still feel this way? Like I am slowly dying from the inside out. I have no energy, no motivation, and happiness is in short supply. This pain is getting real old. I am irritable, fatigued, angry, depressed, and empty.

It seems the inevitable has happened - I have slid back to where I was before. But did I really leave that place, or did I just put a Band-Aid on a gunshot wound?

- XV

Down II
May 31st

I don't know what to do. She is depressed but will not get help. She says she can barely talk to me about it, let alone a counsellor. I feel helpless. I know just how deep and dark the unforgiving void of depression is, and she is dangerously close to falling in. Part of me understands that she has anxiety about talking to people, and maybe can't articulate what she is feeling... But another part of me wants to shake her and scream at her to get help before she becomes like me. She says she has felt this way for a long time, but I can't help but wonder if my illness has brought out hers. I know it sounds self-absorbed, but history shows that I have a damaging effect on those around me. One of my exes slashed her wrists in front of me trying to kill herself, another cut her body up every day... Did I do this?

Either way, I want to help her, but I can't push her into anything. All I can do is be here for support to keep her from falling down. But am I strong enough? I don't think I am, but I am sure as Hell going to try. It's a helpless feeling that makes me sick to my stomach. I am on my way down, and she may be too. What is it with me and chaos?

Fuck

- XV

Drained
June 1st

I feel drained. Like the energy has been sapped from my body and mind. I feel angry, irritable, and empty. Like a hollow vessel going through the motions of life. I walk around spaced out, not really there. Motivation has escaped me and I don't know what's going to happen. I keep saying I can't go back to old ways, but this is feeling like deja vu. I don't know what else to say or do. This is exhausting. I feel lost. Even typing these words is difficult, not only to think but to make my fingers work. Fuck.

- XV

My Body Is A Cage
June 6th

My body is a cage. Inside, it feels like a feral animal is clawing and screaming for release. Yet I supress it. I had come to the revelation years ago that I would not censor, I would not filter, I would not change because societal norms said so... And here I am. To quote myself, I am "being a good little robot". On the outside, yes. On the inside, no. Has the person who declared war against society really disappeared, or has he been shut out and stifled because life is easier that way? I feel like a pendulum, moving back and forth between two extremes. One extreme will almost certainly destroy me, the other will see me succeed. The choice seems obvious, doesn't it? It's not so simple, unfortunately. I am unhappy still. Going to school, working, fighting the urge to give in to my Demons... It all feels wrong. Why, with so much progress made in my life, am I still miserable? Sure, the highs were synthetic, but they were the only time I could let go. The only time that life didn't seem so pointless and tedious.

Reading back on previous entries from years ago (which I have now published into a book, that may or may not see the light of day), I seemed to be more self-confident, more sure that the path I was on was the right one. Now, I am filled with uncertainty, and the old me seems to be coming back. Drugs, sex, recklessness, depression, anxiety, and sleeplessness are becoming more prevalent in a life I had worked so hard to fix. Now I wonder if it even needed fixing. I need to cut out the comparisons to the 'norms', because surely by now you know I HATE that word. What is normal? What is socially acceptable? Then can I argue that normality is doing what you need to in order to make yourself happy? Well, drugs made me happy, yet that is against the grain. I suppose that in itself is a weak argument.

It just seems no matter how hard I fight, inevitably I end up feeling like shit, doubting myself, doing drugs, and falling back into old mindsets and habits. Maybe I am destined to be the way I was years ago, broken and unsalvageable. I am so sick of doing what I think will make others happy. Now, if I go back to old ways, all Hell would break loose. I am torn. It is exhausting. So what the fuck do I do? It is a shitty position, being stuck between unhappiness and happy unhappiness. At least before I could numb all this shit regularly with pills and powder.

Am I just too cowardly to face the challenges of life (mostly) sober? Am I too broken from my past to be able to function as a member of society?

I can feel myself slipping, and it's only a matter of time before I fall.

- XV

Cyclic
June 8th

I feel the repetition getting to me. The upswings and downswings repeating over and over; an endless loop of misery and brief happiness that seems to never end. Yesterday, for example, I went to a Toronto Blue Jays game and was in a great mood, happily cheering them on, forgetting my troubles, my pain, and getting a glimpse of an unfamiliar feeling. Sure enough, not long after (the drive home, actually), my mood dropped like a rock. I was irritable and felt empty and depressed. I am capable of happiness, but it only seems to be frustratingly temporary. Inevitably, I fall back to feeling like shit, leaving me worse off than before. It leads me to wonder if on those rare occasions I am truly happy, or if it is something else. What it is, I don't know. It seems all too brief to be real.

It's been hard not being able to see my counsellor regularly. I just don't have the money for it, even though it helps. That's the bullshit part of it. Finances keep me from getting help, and I sink lower. The medication can only do so much on its own, and it isn't enough.

I have little to no motivation to do anything. Life seems tedious and it truly wouldn't bother me is it all fell apart and I went back to how I was three years ago. Do people change? Maybe. That person, that broken mess, is still inside me. The pieces are just taped together into something resembling a human. I feel empty. I have for years, and despite all the changes in my life, that has stayed the same. I feel like I can never get back everything I lost during those dark years of my life. How can I gain back what was so violently destroyed? How can I rebuild myself, my soul, my mind when they have been poisoned, cut up, and smashed time and time again? Maybe I can't. Maybe I am fucked. All the king's horses and all the king's men would be hard-pressed to fix the damage I have done to myself.

- XV

The Quintessential Depressive
June 9th

Last night my mood dropped lower than it has in a long time. I felt empty, hopeless, and alone - The Quintessential Depressive. The pills are doing nothing and counselling is out of the question for the most part. I am too stubborn to seek free counselling because they don't know me like the one I see now does. I first saw her in 2010 when shit was really beginning to hit the fan. I don't want to have to go over my life history with another shrink, recounting the extensive history of my mental illness. It's too much, and frankly I have a hard time remembering a lot of it due to drugs and repression. The only way I can get an idea of my life back then is through my written journals. Reading those scares me. It was a dark, empty person who wrote those words, and as I've said before, I worry that He is still in there. I'm worried He is making a comeback now. I'm just worried.

I've beat this before, and can likely do it again. I'm just so exhausted. I'm sick of not being able to sleep, feeling empty and depressed, not being able to eat, and all the other bullshit that comes with my condition. I want it gone, but it is a harsh reality that I will never truly be rid of this sickness. There is no cure and no catharsis. The damage I have done to myself has left me barely intact. I am tired of fighting every single day to hold the pieces together, fighting another collapse. I'm just tired.

What I feel is hard to articulate. That's the reason I have over 700 pages of written journals and almost two books worth of online journals - I am struggling to understand what is happening to me. Maybe there is no explanation. Maybe it's just who I am. If my pain is to inevitably continue, maybe there is little I can do to stop it. I grow weak fighting the same battle day after day, fighting my Demons, holding the darkness back... Soon, the levee may break and with it will come a flood of hate, anger, and chaos that will destroy me and those around me.

Or maybe I'm just being dramatic... Who knows?

- XV

Writer's Block
June 21st

I have severely slacked on keeping this journal up to date. Work has been crazy, life has been moving fast, and I really just have nothing to say of note. I am still struggling with my mood, and I feel like I am losing the battle to keep my head above water. Of course it isn't all bad. I got a promotion of sorts at work and will be making a LOT of money for 6 weeks while I cover someone who is going on sick leave. My relationship is great, and the distance doesn't seem to be causing the same problems as it was before. However, these good things don't seem to stop the poisonous fog from rolling in and suffocating me. It will happen randomly, going from a great mood to complete shit in a matter of minutes, and the few times my girlfriend has experienced this, I have been hard-pressed to explain it. I honestly don't know why this happens. Biology can only explain so much, and sometimes the depression simply overwhelms me. I hate that I am this way. I hate that I am back to taking anti-depressants that don't seem to be working all that well. I hate not being able to see my counsellor weekly because I cannot afford it. Pills on their own will not help, and not having someone to talk to (professionally) is hard. In September, it will be free to see my counsellor again, and until then, I have to pay $100 per visit if I really need to go.

I guess I am just plugging away, surviving, fighting to keep balance and the monster at bay. Life shouldn't be this way, but this was the shit-covered hand I was dealt, so I must deal with it. I have beaten this before (barely) and I can probably beat it again, but doubt still whispers in my ear about how strong I really am. For BPD, the prognosis is rarely a good one. With a 10% mortality rate, usually by suicide, and no way to cure it (not to mention the concurrent mood disorders), I am stuck. Most likely this will be my life. Okay, bad, okay, bad - a cycle that will end only with my own end. That is probably what causes the 10% - hopelessness. A feeling that no matter what you do, the crushing weight of this disorder will always be on your back, threatening to push your head below water and slowly drown you.

So I fight on, against the piss and the shit, against my very nature, trying to achieve a life I can bear. Happiness shouldn't be some unachievable goal, but something tells me that with the chronic emptiness I feel, it is somewhere approaching unachievable. Maybe I am wrong... Maybe not.

- XV

At A Loss For Words
June 22nd

Sometimes I just don't get it. As I said in a previous post, my mood can change from high to low in a matter of minutes. Today was no exception. I don't know what the fuck is wrong with me, but I know that if I keep this up, she will not always be so understanding. I hate when I am asked what is wrong and I cannot find the words to articulate the unbearable pain I feel inside. Sometimes it gets too much, and no word in any language can sum it up. Shit is a word that I use a lot to describe my mood, but it rarely does it any justice. Empty is the closest, yet still seems lacking in it's definition. I don't know what I can do or say that will make her, or anyone, understand what I am feeling.

I wish I could just show her, let her peek inside my mind, into the chaos and the horror to get a glimpse of what makes me the way I am. Maybe that wouldn't be such a good thing. Maybe that mystery, the questions she has that I cannot answer are what keep her around. Maybe if some truths were to get out, she would see me in a different light. Not truths about what I have done, but truths like this pain will be with me for life. Truths like some days I wonder why I even try, wonder how I am still alive... and why. Ugly truths that are simply the realities of one who has lived in a state of depressive chaos for years.

But of course, I cannot. I am left, instead, with the inability to enable her to understand. I barely understand myself most of the time. I stumble through each crisis, each depressed mood on the basic knowledge I have gathered and the hopes that this time I won't completely fuck everything up - something I am all too famous for doing. I find myself at a crossroads, wondering if I am really ready for this relationship. I want to be, I want it with every fibre of my being. However I cannot ignore the obvious - I am damaged. I will likely damage her, and for that I could never forgive myself. She means the world to me but sometimes I cannot show her that, even at times when it matters the most.

She often sends me articles on what it is like for a shy, socially awkward person - something she sees herself as, and probably is (love her anyways). I can only wish that an article could be written that shows her the struggles of someone with BPD, or any mental illness. I have let her read a year of my journal entries, against my better judgment. But that barely scratches the surface. I am nowhere near articulate enough to define how I feel, what I think, or why my actions often don't match my feelings. I do not use my illness as a crutch, but often it is hard to come up with any other explanation. Sometimes my behaviour is simply a by-product of my condition. Sometimes it IS the best reason. And sometimes it isn't.

- XV

All Messed Up With Nowhere to Go
June 25th

It seems like forever ago, a different life, where I was more monster than man. The written journals dating back several years are a testament to my psychosis. I was so far detached from reality that I had created my own little world. One full of chaos and despair, full of dread and misery, full of sex, drugs, and rock n roll. I would do so many drugs that the hallucinations became real to me. My attempt to escape reality was a resounding success, and even went further than I had intended, or even realized at the time. I would hallucinate demons out to get me, shadowy figures who told me to self-destruct, and people from a different life whom I once loved. At the time, I didn't give a shit that it was not good for me (to say the least). I didn't care about destroying myself because that was my goal - self-destruction.

It seems like a different life where I was high every day to escape the pain. Where I was alone, abandoned by those I once loved. Can I blame them? No. They should have ran sooner, but their love for me gave them hope that I could beat the disease that threatened my life. It wasn't until years later that I got better. I am not well, even today, but I have things under control that I never thought I would. Though the depression still plagues me and the thoughts of chaos can be overwhelming, I feel stronger from what I went through and weaker at the same time.

That fateful night where I decided to end it all took a lot from me, and I will never get that back. I can never be as complete as I was before. I can only hope the part of me that died that day was one that was poisoned. After that happened, my family made frantic efforts to get me into a treatment centre. I made the joke that I was "all messed up with nowhere to go", however they failed to see the humor in that. Again, I don't blame them. There must be nothing worse than watching someone you love, especially one of your children, give up on life and throw everything away for substance. To see disease take hold and turn them into some unrecognisable monster Hell-bent on self-destruction.

An earmark of BPD is chaos. I thrived in chaotic situations, jumping from girl to girl, drug to drug - all the while watching the pandemonium created by my actions. In hindsight, it was childish and only served to hurt those around me (something I regret to this day).

The battle rages on inside me. Sometimes the Dark whispers, begs to be released once more, yet more times than not the Light wins. I know I am not cured, and to say the Dark is gone or even diminished is ridiculous. The biggest change is that I have learned to control the Dark (mostly). I have found ways to cope, alternatives to self-destructive behaviour, and most of all I have found a new respect for those I love.

It was messy, disturbing, grotesque, obscene... but it led me to where I am now. Although I still have my fair share of Demons, I have learned from the past and continue to move forward, something I hope everyone suffering from a mental illness can achieve.

- XV

Point
June 26th

The point of this journal is not just to vent, rationalize, or get my thoughts out... It is that maybe someday someone who suffers from mental illness will read it and no longer feel so alone. I want to write the kind of thing that if I read it during my worst times, I wouldn't feel like I was the only one; that no one understood my pain. Though many of the previous entries are not exactly optimistic and inspirational, they are true. It is a unique look into the mind of someone society has deemed 'mentally ill'. Though I do not argue with such a verdict, I believe it to be an oversimplification. Everyone is unique, has their own story, their own personality, and their own symptoms. Despite the differences the 'mentally ill' feel, we can take solace in knowing we are not alone.

The road to recovery is treacherous. I won't lie - there are some of us that never recover. Sometimes a happy ending just isn't in the cards. It is a lifelong battle, never ceasing, never cured, only constant. The difference is how you react to it. Do you let it consume you? Kill you? Break you? Make you stronger? Build character? Toughen you up? Change your world view? Well, that depends... on you.

The resources available to the mentally ill are extensive. We have come a long way from locking people in cages, to exorcisms, and to lobotomies. The stigma exists, but people are starting to understand that it is a serious problem, one with no cure and the potential for disaster. It is hard to reach out for help, especially when you don't think you want it or would benefit from it. Try. Fight. Beat the Demons down until they have no more power on you. I have, for the most part. I learned to cope and to deal with the bullshit as it comes, in a way that won't end in my death.

I have yet to find catharsis. It may never come. But I do have tools that make this horrible, unforgiving mental disorder manageable. Chin up, there's always hope.

- XV

Find My Way
June 29th

I have spent my life searching. Searching for who I am, who and what I am supposed to be, what brings me happiness, and of course the perfect high. I have searched the light, fought for a life where I was happy and successful, and failed. I stumbled around in Purgatory, the place between light and dark... Until I chose a new path. I have been to every dark recess of my mind (that I am aware of) looking for the answer, however I found mostly pain. Mostly. I also found a place where I was some synthetic form of happy. A world like Alice's 'Wonderland' where reality was an abstraction. It was whatever the fuck I wanted it to be and I thrived. The real world around me crumbled as I built my Wonderland, but I did not care. Real people left, replaced by imaginary beings that haunted me endlessly.

It was what could only be called psychosis. Whether it was brought on by my illness or by drugs I may never know, but I do know that despite the damage it was doing to my life, I learned to embrace it. Dark became my identity and I was more of a 'thing' than a man. Endless nights in my room, lines of white powder neatly laid out before me, a straw in one hand and a razor in the other. Pill bottles littered the table and it would be as dark as I could make it without being completely blind. I would shake uncontrollably, both from the drugs and from the pain I inflicted upon myself. I figured I deserved it. She must have thought so. Why else would she destroy my life?

There is nothing more dangerous than your own mind. It is a trickster, it dwells... remembering the things you want to forget and forgetting those you want to remember. It holds your deepest fears and seems to let them trickle out when you let your guard down. It knows all your sins, and the guilt is torture. The mind I was prized, academic and logical, was being torn apart. Thoughts of pain and death would tear holes in my psyche, hallucinations made me question reality, and who I was at the most basic level was changing. I was barely human at the worst of it all. I recently read a journal entry from a few years back where I was convinced my room was haunted by myself and those I had hurt. I was scared to close my eyes to sleep so the drugs kept me awake.

I don't know exactly when it all changed. It could have been when I cut up my arm so bad the doctor could barely stitch it back together. Or the overdose where I nearly lost my liver, or the lead poisoning I gave myself that put me in the ICU, or the night I took a bag full of ecstasy and spent the night running from imaginary SWAT teams in the pouring rain ... I could go on but I think the point has been made. Rock bottom was quite a climb just to get to. Something in me changed, didn't want the pain and the bullshit anymore. I wanted a future, but I had to fight hard to convince myself that I really did. If it wasn't for the help of family, I surely would have died in my room - bloody, poisoned, and broken.

So I applied for College. A simple one-year certificate program, but it was something to get my shattered mind working again and a way to pick up the pieces of my life. Don't get me wrong, it was not an easy ride. I struggled with drugs a bit, with the thoughts, with sleep... but for the first time in years I was moving forward. I had a goal. That was big.

At this moment, as I type these words, I am far from free of the burdens from my disorder and the sins of my past, but I feel better equipped to handle the shit life enjoys tossing at you. The memories of what I went through will never go away, nor will the scars (despite wasting money on laser treatment), and in a way I am glad they won't. They are a part of me now. I will never be the same, but hey, maybe that's a good thing.

I'm just trying to find my way.

- XV

The Beginning of (Almost) the End
July 1st

I have written lengthy posts about my pain and misery, about my descent into madness, about my addictions, and about what I have lost. But what I have not posted about is how it all began. So, here it is:

I was one of the top students in my high school and when I received my acceptance letter to one of the best universities in Canada, I could not have been more excited. I had a plan, a mission, and I was determined to stick to it. The first year of university went well, despite struggling with the course load and perhaps a bit too much partying. Second year, however, was a different story.

It started much like the first year, but that lasted only a month and a half. It was mid-October of 2009 that things changed. I didn't know it at the time, but this was the beginning of years of pain and agony that would nearly kill me. My roommates noticed the shift in my behaviour even before I did. I was sleeping about thirteen hours a night (and day), missing classes, not eating, and not socializing. I was irritable and disconnected. It went on like that for a few weeks before the 'intervention' came.

My roommates sat me down and asked what was going on. I had no answer. It hadn't dawned on me that I was changing. Sure, I had slight problems with my mood and sleep in the past, and as I have said in previous posts, I was no stranger to drugs. It was then that I realized something in me was shifting, akin to a cloud slowly covering the sun.

They convinced me to see a doctor at the university clinic. It took her just five minutes to ask me a few basic questions and write a prescription for an anti-depressant. That was it – drugs, but no counselling or any other treatment. Let me digress for a second and point out this fundamental flaw in our mental health system. Doctors are so quick to diagnose based on only a few questions, with only a three week history of depressive symptoms, then write out a prescription and send the patient on their way. Anyway, back to the story.

I began my 'treatment' and didn't have very high hopes for the outcome. I felt empty, tired beyond description, confused, depressed, and hopeless. At the time the diagnosis made me angry. I felt like if this was what was really happening, I would be letting down my family, especially if I had to leave university. In hindsight, it wasn't true. They were there for me no matter what.

My mind was racing and the thoughts were driving me crazy. They made it even harder to sleep as my hypersomnia had turned into insomnia. Why? No clue. MY solution was to begin journaling in the vain hope that not only would it clear some of the racing thoughts out of my head, but that it would also allow me to make sense of what was happening to me. These feelings were new and I had absolutely no idea how to deal with them or even understand them.

The journals worked, to some extent, but also made my condition worse. I poured my soul into them and it caused me to focus on the negative instead of the positive (however little there was). To this day, I still have them – over 700 pages chronicling the worst years of my life. It is hard to look back at them, and I tend not to. They sit in my drawer serving no purpose but to be used to remember dates and events that, due to heavy drug use, I cannot remember.

About three weeks after these symptoms started, and only a few days after the start of my anti-depressant treatment, I wrote:

"For the last 3 weeks I have been plagued with depression. Nothing is good anymore. Every breath is like poison and every movement drains the energy from my body... I sit alone in my room for hours on end – numb, empty."

That post was from November 3rd where I really began to notice that who I used to be was being replaced by something much more sinister.

By the time I was forced to leave university because of my illness, I had switched anti-depressants due to an adverse reaction to the first one and been put on anxiety medication.

After returning home, things did not improve. My condition continued to decline to the point where I was hospitalized for cutting and taking too many pills. This wouldn't be the last time I attempted self-destruction, and the years to come would be the worst of my life (so far). I hope that I will never have to feel that way again. I wouldn't wish this on anyone.

So there it is, a very brief history of how it all began. Nothing triggered it and there was no concrete diagnosis until years later. Moral of the story is, sometimes the symptoms are not so obvious. Sometimes it takes a friend or family member to tell you that you are changing. Don't ignore the symptoms if they come, because it does not take too long for shit to get really out of control.

- XV

Sinister
July 2nd

What the fuck is wrong with me? Today, I hit a point lower than I have hit in a while. I saw my therapist, and even that didn't help. I had this feeling in the pit of my stomach, like something dark and sinister was clawing at my insides to escape. I felt pure emptiness and pain like I have not felt in a long time. I was bitter and cold with her, taking everything she said as an attack, despite the obvious fact she was trying to help me.

Then it continued with my girlfriend. When I got home we talked on the phone and the dark feeling grew. I felt an inexplicable and overwhelming sadness taking over, and though I was aware it was happening, I was helpless to stop it. The feeling of emptiness is chronic, but today it reached a high point. One part of me was angry, bitter, cold, hateful; while the other was desperately trying to fight off those negative emotions. It was an internal battle that drained me. I am scared that history will repeat itself; that she will see that my unpredictable mood swings can be catastrophic to our relationship and she will leave me, like the others.

But I know she is not like the others, which makes this better and worse at the same time. She may not leave, but I cannot make her deal with this. I cannot bring her down with my bullshit. I love her way too much to drag her down into the fiery pit of Hell I often call home. She is my only salvation from the suffering, and I cannot lose her. I want to be the man she deserves, I want to give her everything, every part of me and show her that she is truly amazing.

I need to fix things, and fast. She is coming to visit for the weekend tomorrow, and I know that it will be tough at first, but just being able to hold her in my arms will be the best defense against the Darkness that knocks at my door. I love you babe. I will be strong for you.

- XV

Bring You Down
July 4th

Today was proof that you bit off more than you can chew. We talked today, really talked. Got the ugly truth out and now we have to face it. Demons from past and present haunt us both more than I could have ever imagined. I have so much fucking baggage that I wonder if involving you in the shit-storm that us my life is really worth it.

Then, of course, I remember how much I love you. Selfishly, I go ahead and push down my Demons so that we can be 'us'. As you lay beside me asleep, I am kept awake wondering if I will only end up hurting you like all the others. You deserve the best, and I want to give it to you. I do. I just think too much of me has been destroyed already. I truly hope I am wrong.

- XV

Ticking Time Bomb
July 5th

I call myself a ticking time bomb because I feel so unstable that at any moment I can explode. I walk a fine line between right and wrong, stepping into one side more than the other from time to time. Only so much can be blamed on my condition, and I need to own up to my actions. However it cannot be ignored that my thoughts and actions are often textbook BPD. I guess I also walk a line between explanation and excuse, constantly wondering which is true.

There is a lot of pressure for me to do the 'right thing', say the 'right thing', make the 'right choice'… but what about what I want? From high school the pressure was on to get into university and get a degree, then perhaps medical school. That failed, so the pressure was on to figure out what went wrong, what mental illness was plaguing me, and to get better. Once I started to get better, the pressure was on to look at school again. I went, finished a one-year certificate program and the pressure was on again to get a degree. A bachelor's degree in nursing, only because I was told that with my criminal record, it was likely the only thing I could do in medicine. Of course, it wasn't. I got a call to the Dean's office and I was out of the program. Then the pressure was on to land on my feet and go right into another program.

So here I am, in yet another program, with little time to breathe between choices, no time to think things through, just the pressure to act, and act fast. Sure, I need to do something. I was set pretty far back due to my illness, but sometimes it feels like too much. On top of the academic pressures are the pressures at work, the pressures to stay clean, to be happy, to stay on track, to be the person my girlfriend wants me to be, and who she deserves.

I feel like I am suffocating sometimes under the pressure, and one day I may explode in a supernova of resentment, anger, and self-destruction. I am a firm believer that the person from four years ago who cut his wrists to the point the doctor could barely sew it back together is still inside. I feel like it would not take much to devolve into my old ways. But I am not supposed to. It's not right.

The reason behind all this pressure is the fact I have potential. I am smart and I can do great things if I put my mind to it. Does that automatically mean I should? Apparently. I am not saying that I should just be a fuck-up and do nothing with my life, but I am saying that I have a choice in all of this.

I truly do not know what I want. I may never know. I have not had time to think about it because everything has been happening so fast. I am 25 years old, still struggling to find my way, and I have no fucking clue what my future holds. The life-expectancy of those with my condition is low, especially along with my smoking and substance use. I may have already lived half my life and currently have very little to show for it.

- XV

Aggressive Depressive
July 6th

Lately I have been feeling hateful and angry. Little things get to me more than they should and worse than they usually do. I have felt depressed to the point where I have no energy, no motivation, and no fucks to give. How is this different than usual, you ask? Well dear readers, it seems to be more pronounced now. It seems to be the worst it has been in a while.

I opened up to my girlfriend on the weekend in a way I told myself I never would. Some of my deepest, darkest secrets came out this weekend and it is a door I can never close. I may never know what she truly thinks about what I said, and maybe it is better that way. But she also told me something that was equally devastating. I am so used to being caught up in all my problems and bullshit that I forget that I need to be empathetic and realize that there may be things going on in her (or someone else's) life that equals or trumps my own.

I have a good idea of how to deal with my issues... for the most part. I recently learned that I have NO idea how to deal with someone I care deeply about. It is painful when you don't have the right words to say to make things better. It cuts deep when you feel like there is no way to help them. All I can do is use my extensive experience and use what works for me and hope it applies to her.

Back to what I 'spilled' on the weekend, it was mostly about the sins of my past. The horrible things I have seen and done; things from the past that still haunt me to this day. Unfortunately, these things still occupy a rather large piece of real estate in my mind and no matter what I do I cannot seem to let go. Some days I do not think about them, but some days they crush me like the day they happened. These things have changed me. Some of these things were precursors to what would become my fall to rock bottom. Some were a result of being so low.

I beat my head against the wall wishing things were different. I fucking hate that I feel like shit, that I feel depressed and empty, that I use drugs to numb the pain, and that every shitty thing I have done still disturbs me to this day. I cannot seem to escape this cycle, and if just learning to live with it is my only option, sometimes I wonder if it is worth it. Sometimes my Dark Passenger speaks louder than others, insisting that I give up and let myself fall. I have come a long way, but in many ways, I am still essentially the same. How much can one really change? That seems to be the million dollar existential question that keeps me up at night.

- XV

Insomnia Aplenty
July 7th

It is currently 1:00am and I cannot sleep, despite 8mg of clonazepam, two sleeping pill, and a bottle of wine. I can't take much more of this bullshit. I see my doctor on Wednesday, so I guess technically tomorrow seeing as it is 1:00am Tuesday morning. I need to be up in 6 hours for work, and sleep doesn't even seem to be on the horizon. It's not just because my mind racing, and my body and mind certainly are exhausted; to be honest, I have no fucking clue what this is. The pills I took would knock the average person out for a good 12 hours. So why no relief?

Sleep has always eluded me, and no matter what meds I am prescribed, I always seem to gain a tolerance quickly. I don't know what answers the doctor will have for me tomorrow, but I hope he can do SOMETHING for me. I have tried just about every pill there is for sleep – both on-label and off-label, prescribed and non-prescribed. My doctor has been amazingly patient despite watching me spiral out of control, abusing the prescriptions he wrote for me (back in the day, not so much anymore), and coming to him for years, desperately trying to find some solution to my illness.

I always seem to get my hopes up, but having tried so much, I am not sure how much he can really do. He is a GP, not a specialist in this kind of stuff. The psychiatrists I have seen locally, or anywhere for that matter, have been terrible. No bedside manner, no time for you, and one even went as far as to say, "I am only here to give you meds, not hold your hand". Fucker.

Wish me luck on yet another appointment dedicated to finding some way to achieve one of the most basic human functions – sleep. My hopes for a solution aren't too high, but I do hope I am wrong.

- XV

Building an Audience
July 7th

I have spent the last few days finding ways to promote my first book. It is so hard to get started, and sometimes I wonder if it is even worth it. I truly want to help people like me and I hope that I am able to do it.

Textbooks can define each mental illness, give the characteristic symptoms, and the usual treatment. What they lack is emotion. I have poured my soul into these entries and I hope that in doing so people will better understand mental illness. I want to write something that if I had read years ago, it may have saved me a lot of pain.

I am not looking to write a masterpiece capable of curing people's ailments, but if I can make a difference in someone's life, I will be happy. This is going to be a long and hard road, but if I can accomplish what I am aiming for, it will be all worth it in the end.

- XV

Off To See the Doctor
July 8th

I see my doctor in 45 minutes. I will beg him for a better sleeping pill. Beg. This cannot go on much longer or I am going to lose my mind!!! Here's hoping for the best. I will update tonight after the appointment and hopefully it will be good news.

He has seen me go through some rough shit - shit most doctors will never see. Yet he keeps fighting for me. He has been my doctor since I was born, and I know he cares deeply, which is hard to find in a doctor these days, unfortunately. I know he will listen, understand, and do the best he can to help me out. I don't know what medication will work for me, but hopefully he has a few ideas.

I cannot go on like this much longer.

- XV

Try and Try Again
July 8th

My visit to the doctor went alright. He was receptive to my desire to stop taking the sleeping pill I am currently on that doesn't work and try a new one. However, it isn't really a 'new' one. I have tried this medication in the past, but I don't quite remember how well it worked. I have been on so many fucking medications it is hard to keep track of all the names and the effects they had on me. So we will try this one again and see what happens.

He gave me a flexible dose, meaning I can start with half of one and work my way up to two if necessary. Judging by my history of insane tolerances to drugs, I will certainly not start at half, especially with how little sleep I have had in the last few weeks.

I start my new job tomorrow. Same place, different job title, and **much** better hourly wage. I am nervous and excited at the same time, and I hope I can do well and not get too stressed about the increased workload and lack of training.
I have felt so disconnected lately, sort of like I used to be – going through the motions but with my heart not really being in it. I find it hard to focus and to care about things. Maybe it is the lack of sleep that is making me this way, which will hopefully be remedied by this prescription. I just feel hostile, and that along with the fatigue and chronic emptiness is an ugly mix. At least I can see my councillor tomorrow and talk some things out.

- XV

Sleep At Last
July 9th

The new pills worked! I took two, but probably should have started with one. I was really groggy when I woke up this morning, so tonight I will take just one a little bit earlier and hopefully not have the hangover feeling tomorrow morning.

The new job is stressful, but with the money I'm making, I will not complain... too much. People just need to simmer the fuck down. The work will get done, and the work I'm doing I have never done before. Despite that, I think I am doing pretty well, especially with barely any training.

Otherwise not much else is going on. At least nothing noteworthy. Maybe I will think of something later.

- XV

Nostalgia
July 10th

I've done a lot of looking back lately, trying to remember details of my life that seem like they happened a million years ago. The overdoses, the cutting, the week-long binges, the countless nights alone in drug-induced psychosis, and countless other acts of depravity that defined my life. Maybe it's better to leave the past in the past, but for some reason I need to remember. I seem to have supressed so much, or maybe just can't remember because of all the drugs... either way I read my old journals and find things that still shock me to this day.

Take this journal entry, for example. I wrote it on September 23rd, 2011 during a very rough time (to say the least). I was so close to giving up, to letting go and ending it all. It seems like forever ago.

"24 hours into this coke bender, I realize just how much I am flirting with death. The next line could finally shut my heart down. The shakes are the worst I've ever had. Paranoia is setting

in and I can't help but wonder if my next breath could be my last. How long will my lifeless body lay here in my apartment until someone finally realizes I'm dead? Could be days, with the lack of social contact I have. Does it worry me enough to stop? No, but it should. Have I finally pushed my body over the edge? I guess I'll have to wait and see. That doesn't help the anxiety, shakes, and paranoia I feel coming. Here I go..."

Clearly I didn't really care about my well-being then, but some part of me seemed to hold on to the hope that I could change, and maybe even get better. I was so far down in the pit that it all seemed so hopeless and redundant. That particular experience had me awake for almost two days straight, going through about six grams of cocaine, and beginning to hallucinate ghostly figures in my room.

In the next few months I started a methadone treatment to fight my drug addiction, and as I figured from the start, that didn't last either. I was cut off due to positive drug testing. I fooled them for a while, taking only certain drugs in certain doses so they wouldn't show up in my system. Things like Concerta, an amphetamine that you could snort, pop, or inject – all of which I did at least once.

By the end of December I had started and destroyed a relationship and only seemed to be getting more hopeless and depressed, a feat that I imagined impossible. By the New Year, 2012, my depression had turned to anger. I was aggressive and hostile, lashing out at any who had burned me or disappeared from my life. It was a terrible way to live, to say the least. The constant pain was destroying me from the inside, turning me into some unrecognizable monster that became more repulsive with each passing day.

Looking back may not be good for me, but it does let me see how far I have come. All that being such a distant memory is reassuring. Though I am still a work in progress, I have fought for years against a beast that no one can understand, and as of now, I am winning. Mental illness is Hell, pure and simple. For some, it will be their undoing and their demise, for others, it is a true test of their will to live and heal. Sadly, many succumb to their illness, but there is a majority that fight with unrelenting power and beat their sickness. I have not won yet, but I am certainly in a much better place than I was just three years ago.

- XV

Nostalgia II
July 13th

I lay in bed, for the third night in a row where sleep has been more difficult than is has been in a while. It completely and utterly escapes me as my mind races about anything and everything and nothing at all. It is amazing how fast sleep deprivation can fuck you up. In only a few nights I have become inattentive and whacked out during the day. Tonight doesn't seem like it is going to be any different than the past few nights.

So I decided to write another entry looking back. At the time I wrote this on February 3rd, 2012, I knew that this entry would be hard to write. It took a lot for me to do as well as a lot from me. I have altered the entry somewhat to protect people I have named (against my usual policy of transparency). The names have been changed to something completely ridiculous to cover my ass, not theirs:

"I've spent the last hour looking back on my life, trying to figure out what the fuck happened. Going into second year of university I was fine. Then - BOOM! My mood drops and I began my long fall. It has been over two years now and yet it seems like a lifetime. I've tried to end my life more than a few times, and I've broken many hearts.

Crazy was the one who pulled the trigger on my life. I believe she is the reason I came home (from university). Her depression felt like my fault and I needed to make it right. So I came home. I came home to Crazy telling me of kidney failure and embracing death. I watched as the life literally poured out of her, but no one cared that I saved her on that cold December night. I think we both died in our own way that night. I was blamed, yet I clung on the torn fabrics of a love that once was.

Scars began to line my body as I punished myself for the pain I'd caused. During this, I found Crazy 2. One who I thought understood and could relate. It turned out to be another imaginary 'forever'. To this day it is tough to say if they even loved me at all, or if I even understood love.
I was charged as spring sprung in 2009. A crime I did not commit, guilty until I gave in and lied to the court (on advice from my douchebag lawyer). The lie was that I was guilty. They had treated me as a criminal for so long I began to believe it. Throughout all this time I felt dead inside. I felt hopeless.

I was alone. I dove into cocaine and nearly lost myself. Like a pendulum, I went back and forth from hating and blaming Crazy and Crazy 2, and hating and blaming myself. I knew all along, as lost in a world of drug-induced psychosis as I was, that I fucked up. I wished I was dead, but I opted to punish myself for this by living with the pain. Every day, since then, I have only know loss, pain, and regret. That is more punishment than anyone should bear.

In no way is it 'better to have loved and lost than never loved at all'. Love is the only thing that can lift you to the Heavens, then slam you into the deepest circles of Hell.

This is one of the most revealing and most painful entry I have put into these journals so far. It had to be done. Despite this, I continue to lack clarity on many aspects of my life. All I know is that I have seen Heaven and I have seen Hell, and I have lived everything in between. Yet I still do not know where I stand, or where I prefer. To know yourself – to truly know yourself, you must live in and experience the Light as well as the Dark.

Life. Death. And every joy, pain, and drug in between. This ride isn't over yet..."

So there you have it. During this time, I was at one of my lowest points. I was miserable, alone, stoned, and broken. I was convinced I was beyond repair. Let this be another example that even though you may feel like death is your only out, or that things will never get better, they can. Not in every case, but in most.

Depression is emptiness, suffocating, horrific, shattering, and will sap the energy out of your body. I sit here now while I should be sleeping (I can't anyway) reflecting on a life that went from good, to shitty, to great. I still have my struggles (*ahem* sleep *ahem), however being broken down to nothing has, ironically, allowed me to build myself up stronger and better than before.

- XV

Fast-Forward
July 27th

It feels like my life is flying by. Working this new job has been great, but a true test of both my skill and patience. I guess once the pay cheques come in it will all be worth it, but between that, my upcoming psychology exam, and the nice weather, I have clearly neglected this journal. It has been two weeks since I last posted, and frankly I haven't had much time to think about what is going on inside my head.

Sleep has been easier because at the end of the day I am physically and mentally exhausted. My relationship is better than ever and I count myself lucky every day to be with someone so amazing. Despite all this, I still have that feeling in my chest like there is a profound part of me that is missing. The chronic emptiness is always there, a dull ache that reminds me of my condition. That may never go away, and I have accepted that. I lost a lot over the last few years and because of that, I wouldn't expect myself to ever be whole again.

The big difference is that I no longer (well, not as often) dwell on what is missing and instead turn my focus onto what I have, and what I have is pretty damn good.

Perhaps after work and my course settle down a bit I will have more to write about, but for now it seems like this anti-climactic post is all I can offer. In a way, it sure beats the depressing shit I used to write…

- XV

Flat-Line
August 6th

I sit here at a loss for words. What was once so easy and fluid has become tasking. Maybe it is because my life has become so routine that there is no longer time or space for the things I used to write about. Not having anything to write about does not necessarily mean I feel any better. In fact, it seems my life has become so monotonous that I now rarely feel anything.

Even now I struggle to articulate how I feel. I just feel like I have flat-lined. Everything that makes me who I am has been drained by the repetition of a routine I find lacklustre. I suppose I have always had some form of drama in my life; the absence of which has had a noticeable effect on my writing and mood.

Even talking to my counsellor I found it hard to describe my feelings, simply because I had none to speak of. I feel like Meursault from *The Stranger* by Albert Camus – indifferent and emotionally detached. Lately I have been more of an observer, with no real emotional investment or interest in anything at all.

With this new repetitive life comes an old familiar feeling – the desire for some excitement and recklessness. It is strange, yet I miss (some of) my old life, where at least my indifference was toward myself and I did things that made me feel better. This is a life I could never return to, but the tediousness of my current life has me wishing for excitement and wanting to look for trouble.

But I won't... The new, boring me will continue to be boring. For now.

I guess at this time things are going fairly well, especially when compared to this time two years ago. The pessimist (or realist) in me is, as someone recently told me, 'waiting for the other shoe to drop'. I wonder, with a good job, a great girlfriend, and a relatively good handle on my BPD, what is the catch? Did I finally come out on the other side of the storm? Is this my prize for surviving six years of Hell? Or is this the eye of the storm; a short interlude between acts, where once the curtain opens, the monster inside that I have battled for years will reappear? We shall see.

- XV

Ache
August 10th

I feel run down. Sore. Exhausted. Well, this isn't exactly an extreme deviation from the norm for me, but now it seems more profound.

When I was a teenager, I began having joint pain. The doctor said it was growing pains, however when I was done growing, the pain remained. I saw several specialists, each offering a different answer. A neurologist said it was fibromyalgia, a rheumatologist said rheumatoid arthritis or something like that, and I even had a psychologist tell me the pains were a unique manifestation of OCD – where the ache was my compulsion to move my joints a certain way.

Of course, then came the drugs. First they were prescribed, then inevitably I dipped into non-prescribed drugs. The pain was still there. Now the doctor was certain the pain was all in my head and it was simply my drug-seeking behaviour. Since then I have had the dreaded label of drug-seeker follow me everywhere I go. Sure, it was partially true at the time and I take full responsibility for my actions. The issue was it prevented me from ever getting a proper diagnosis and treatment for my mysterious condition.

So now I live with the pain. Or the compulsions. Or the whatever-the-fuck. It bothers me every day. All day. It never goes away and I suppose I was forced into getting used to it and accepting that it is a permanent part of my life. I lost hope in ever getting an explanation, and I even got to the point (at my lowest) where I convinced myself I deserved the pain. I had to suffer because of who I was and what I had done. But I digress.

Today, it's a chronic, dull ache in my joints where I am (though I am hesitant to use this word) compelled to move them, as if stretching would be a relief. I suppose it could almost be a compulsion. It even gets worse when I am tired, stressed, depressed, or do too much physical activity. I dread writing out essays by hand, and even typing this is aggravating the pain, causing constant stretching and flexing.

I will probably never know what this is, and I still feel disheartened that I ever will. This is the issue I have with the stigma surrounding addiction and mental illness – those labeled as an addict, drug-seeker, mentally ill, or whatever-the-fuck do not receive the same standard of care anyone else would. I won't even go into the number of times I was in pain, having an anxiety attack, or in need of medical attention and I was denied pain medication, anti-anxiety meds, and pretty much anything that could potentially be abused. My doctor is still reluctant to prescribe me a goddamn sleeping pill that would be effective because, holy shit, THEY ARE HABIT FORMING!

My hope is that one day, the stigma will not change what standard of care a patient receives. Maybe the onus is on the medical professionals to diagnose and prescribe properly to avoid abuse. Maybe if my doctors had spent as much time figuring out why I was in pain as they did stamping my medical records with the big, red [DRUG SEEKER] stamp, my desperation would not have led to addiction. But it is not my place to point fingers. Maybes are just that – maybes. Unfortunately, my story resonates with countless people. We are all equally deserving of medical treatment.

Ramble complete. It has been a while.

- XV

Exhaustion
August 12th

I am mentally and physically exhausted. At work I am doing two, sometimes three, people's job plus training (and essentially babysitting) new hires. At home, I am caught in the middle of several wars at once. I am Switzerland, in between warring countries, while simultaneously trying to keep France from giving up and surrendering.

I am starting to feel the weight of everything crushing me. I am constantly on edge, being worn down more and more every day.

It was all I could do today to keep it together at work. To put the metaphorical 'cherry on top' I came home to more problems. It's getting clear that I am losing it, and how much more I can take seems to get less and less with each passing moment.

Something needs to give before this gets out of hand and I fall back into old ways.

- XV

Borderline
August 17th

It feels like I am walking a fine line between sane and insane. The chaos in my life is only building, yet I don't seem to fall over the edge. Maybe after all of these years I have grown accustomed to a life of disorder (pun intended) and living this way is now my 'norm'. Work bullshit, home drama, personal turmoil – it all feels painfully blasé to me. It was for that brief time period not too long ago when things were good that I felt uneasy.

I walked into my counsellor's office, sat down, and for the first time ever I had nothing to say. My job was going well, my relationship even better, home life was stable, and I felt good about myself. Despite this, there was still a voice in the back of my mind asking if it would last. Even my counsellor noticed my cautious approach to this new-found contentment. In her words I was 'waiting for the other shoe to drop'. I argue, however, that there exists a fine line between realism and pessimism – one I carefully tread as a result of my sordid past.

Debaucherous nostalgia aside, I find myself at a crossroads, each direction as ambiguous as the other. Where to go from here is a question I have asked myself a million times, yet always seem unable to lend an answer to. I have had to accept many things in my life as a result of my condition – things that would drive most people to madness – yet the uncertainty is always impossible to embrace. I have never been sure of myself in anything. Leave it to my tortured mind to overthink everything, robbing my conscience of any peace.

Anyway, the existential crisis that is my life continues. A battered psyche trying to push through the poisonous fog in search of a better life, despite the relentless thoughts of certain failure. Sometimes this all seems so pointless. Why wake up when all that awaits me is physical and psychological pain? Why move forward when only misery awaits? Because I have to. I cling on what little I have left, as if I was some hopeless romantic certain I would win my love's affections with persistence. If nothing else, at least I can be called stubborn. If I was too stubborn to die before, I sure as Hell am too stubborn to die now. So what do I do? Endure.

- XV

Anxiety
August 19th

This will be brief. I am not okay. My counsellor took one look at me and knew I was a nervous wreck. Too much is happening at once and I don't know if I am strong enough to go on like this. Eventually, something has to give, and my psyche feels weaker by the day. I have come so far but sometimes it feels like I will never be alright. I seem doomed to live out my life broken and hopeless. There isn't much keeping me anchored now, but what little I have I am holding onto for dear life. It's all I can do, because the alternative... well the alternative is unspeakable. Hold on. Hold on.

- XV

Sedate Me
August 26th

I saw my doctor today, and as soon as he looked at me he knew something was very wrong. He asked me what was going on and I told him. No details, just the main points. He is concerned for my mental health. I don't blame him. Confirmation from both a psychologist and a doctor that this anxiety is eating away at me is hard news to take. I don't know what's worse – the shakes, the constant feeling that my heart will explode, the trouble sleeping, or the fear that this is only the beginning.

This is a familiar feeling. One I have felt more times than I dare to estimate. The anxiety medication he gave me is only a Band-Aid on a gaping wound in my psyche. It seems his hope is for them to do just enough to prevent me from losing it completely. I can make no promises, make no insightful predictions that everything will work out. All I have is this feeling of pure anxiety and dread. Some say history repeats itself. Others say that borderline personality is a death sentence. Others say I'll be just fine.

Place your bets on who is right!

- XV

Recurrence
September 1st

Every once in a while I slip. The mistakes I have made in the past repeat themselves, the lessons I have learned seem to be forgotten, and it feels out of my control. I am one to embrace my nature, despite it sometimes being dark and depraved; but there are certain aspects of my life that I just cannot seem to accept.

I am who I am, and though I believe a person can change their actions and words, who they fundamentally are does not change. As I have said before, the same person that overdosed, that cut his arms to shreds, that spent years taking drugs to numb the pain, and that had all those twisted thoughts is still inside me. I have managed to make profound changes to my life, yet my nature remains constant.

I am tired of being depressed, in pain, constantly fighting the urge to do drugs, battling every night just to sleep, and most of all trying to figure out who the Hell I am. This endless cycle seems destined to repeat itself over and over, driving me insane in the process. Sometimes, the dichotomy of my being is a real bitch, but an vital part of being human... or something like that.

- XV

Time to Fight?
September 2nd

It is over 30 degrees outside, and there I am, walking around with a long-sleeve shirt on. As I walk down the street, sweating my ass off by hiding my shame I wonder – why?

The stigma of having an arm covered in self-inflicted scars is enough to change how I dress to the point of suffering near heat-stroke. At work I do cover them up, more as a professional matter (or so I rationalize it so), but even in public I am very aware that they are there. People tell me they are hard to notice, but to me they stick out like a flashing neon casino sign.

There is, now more than ever, many movements to end the stigma associated with mental illness, scars included. However we are a VERY long way from a paradigm shift in the way people like myself are viewed. It is an innate, instinctual reaction to judge someone quickly; to create an idea of who someone is based on schemas we all have. Generally, wrist-cutting is viewed in a highly negative light.

The truth is that often these scars are a sign of strength, not weakness. They show that this person has been at the lowest point of low, to such an extreme that they cut their own skin – yet they survived. Something inside them made them fight for a life that has frankly dealt them a shitty hand. It is a sign that they have battled upon the precipice of life and death, and survived.

Despite all of this, we still hide our scars in shame. We fear judgement, ridicule, and even abandonment by everyone around us, whether it is rational or not. I dream of a day where I can walk around in a short-sleeved shirt and when someone looks at me, they see strength; a survivor – not weakness. That day is far, far away, and may never come. But I think it is worth fighting for. We cannot ignore a problem that seems to growing exponentially each year.

Until the day where the stigma has all but vanished, I am ashamed to say I will never be comfortable with my scars.

- XV

Pretending
September 3rd

Just keep on pretending that everything is alright, that things will work out in the end – because it is easier that way. The truth is that I am not okay, and the longer that I pretend that isn't true, the worse I am going to get. Holding on to the frayed strings of sanity can only work for so long before I lose my grip.

Listen to me, all negative and shit. This is the only place where I do not have to lie, to put on a mask and pretend that I am okay. I spend so much of my time living a lie that it is draining my energy.

- XV

Shut Down
September 8th

My body has had enough, and it is certainly letting me know. The last months of stress have shot my immune system and now I am paying for it. After pretty bad stomach cramps came insomnia - worse than it has been in a long time. Sore throat, stuffy nose, sneezing, and all that attractive stuff has hit me all at once, and I am not the least bit surprised.

I have put myself through a lot, and with the stresses at work on top of those at home, I am honestly shocked this did not happen sooner. I am simply drained.

My girlfriend is worried, my family is worried, my counsellor is worried, and so is my doctor. Despite these concerns, I seem to lack a sufficient amount of fucks to give about my own well-being. In the past, I would cut and do drugs almost as a punishment to myself for whatever it was I felt guilty about at the time. It seems now I am doing a similar thing to myself where I push myself to the absolute edge of breaking. Why? No clue.

Maybe I am still not over the sins of my past. Maybe I felt I have not suffered enough. Maybe I feel that there are more recent things I need to punish myself for. Or maybe it is just in my nature to be masochistic.

My dreams have been disorganized and crazy lately. I wake up exhausted from them, and despite their lucidity, it is not long before I have forgotten most of the dream and only wisps of images float around in my brain. The dreams seem to be attacking me as well.

I just feel lost and weak. I know I cannot go on like this, but I (for some reason) will not do what is necessary to fix the things in my life that are broken. I fear I have lost all motivation and become a zombie going through the same routine, day after day, until eventually I can no longer function.

I do not want to crumble again. I barely made it back last time. I need to help myself, but I won't.

- XV

A Day to Myself
September 9th

I finally decided to take a day off. That day is tomorrow. Well, I was more pushed into it by those who are seeing me struggle. The house will be quiet so hopefully it really will be a day where I can just relax – no plans, no jobs, no expectations. Could it really be that easy?

There comes a time when even the most self-abusing of people need to take a day off to centre themselves. I can feel the clouds rolling in, and I need to do something to get out of them. Fast.

- XV

Resolution
September 14th

It's becoming clear to me that there are a lot of things that I have been ignoring, feelings that I have pushed down into the darkest recesses of my mind, and brutal truths that I swat away like pesky flies. I can't keep doing that. I, more than most, understand the dangers of the psyche. It's ability to haunt you with a single thought or memory, break you down and bring you to your knees as your own mind turns against you. Warped images of pain and death and horror can flow forth at any time, as if triggered by everything or nothing at all.

Repression cannot lead to resolution, and resolution by no means leads to redemption. What is lost is lost and there is no getting it back. The painful memory of someone or something being torn from you can cascade into a tidal wave of torment and misery, which in turn leads to pain. The pain I would inflict upon myself in the form of blade through skin did nothing to resolve my enraged psyche. The relief was in the punishment, the release felt when blood falls from a wound, and delusion that you are the one controlling the pain.

So now I once again find myself at a crossroads. As I said to my counsellor today, "I open one door and get punched in the face, I open another I get kicked in the nuts." To which she replied,

"But the pain will go away." How I would love to believe her, however my enduring cynicism denies me that belief. It's quite clear a lot can be resolved by a few simple actions. Not *easy* actions, but simple ones. It would seem to cause more pain, yet in the end it may seem well worth it.

When the decision is between a kick to the groin and a haymaker to the face, as a male I see no contest. That does not mean I will enjoy getting punched in the face, though. Now I stumble between choices. What do I do? My future seems hazy and I can't seem to become invested in a potential path. Even this psychology program has me doubting whether it is the right path. I simply have no motivation to move forward.

My only stability is in my girlfriend and my job. The latter will soon change, however. I guess some stability is better than what I have had in the past. Being happy is hard for me and all of this is new to me. Lately I have been getting these feelings of pure, raw depression randomly, with no trigger. It almost incapacitates me, but my 'expertise' in dealing with this old, familiar feeling allows me to push forth. I feel chronically empty; like I am standing on the edge of a colossal, yawning void that is pulling me in slowly. One stumble can destroy me, and it is all too apparent that this fine line I am walking is taking its toll.

Into the fire?

- XV

Then Came You
September 15th

I have been broken for so many years that I forgot what happiness and love really are. The swirling vortex of my condition pulled me under murky waters, choking the life from me until I was a lifeless corpse floating down a river of regret. Love had become synonymous with hate, light with dark, and happiness with impossibility.

Then came you. I had given up on looking for someone. I figured I would only break them and they would only leave me. The idea of love seemed like an abstraction; a fairy-tale used to sell flowers and diamonds. Then I saw you. From first sight, there was something that pulled my gaze to you. I didn't understand why, but I would catch myself staring. Aside from looking like an utter creep, I told myself you looked back a few times.

I carefully navigated my way into a social circle adjacent to yours so that we had to speak, even just a little bit. Before I knew it, I mustered up the courage to ask you out. We sat in that bar and talked for hours... I was hooked.

Ever since then, everything you have said and done has only made me feel surer about being with you. You did the impossible and dragged a broken, love-hating cynic out of the mud and pulled him to his feet. All the pain I had felt before was suddenly worth it as I realized it had brought me to you. I would suffer that pain a thousand times over to be yours. But I don't have to. Even though the pain is still in my mind, and I am still reassembling the fragments of my battered psyche, I have not felt this happy in years.

It takes a special person to look past the scars lining my arms, the pain in my eyes, and the sins of my past to see what could be; to love me for what I am, not what I could or should be. I honestly cannot say that the hard part is behind me now. It certainly will not be smooth sailing from here. This condition is for life. The difference now is that I have you by my side, giving me the strength to fight.

I don't think you know what you do for me; what you mean to me. I could write a million words until my fingers fell off and I still would not scratch the surface. I love you. In every way. I feel undeserving of your love. It's not always easy for me to feel like I deserve something good, but I fight every day to be deserving of you. I always will.

All my love,

- XV

No Catharsis
September 21st

My psychological decline continues, with the turbulent emotions getting worse each day. I feel so close to slipping into a severe depression and I don't know why. I cannot articulate how I am feeling and the reasons why. I am usually very aware of my mental state and the things that effect it. For the first time in a long time, I am utterly depressed and am ignorant to the cause.

I can't help but obsess over the things that make me miserable. I am aware now, more than ever, that this is my life. The BPD, depression, anxiety, and joint pain are a part of me, and that will never change. I am exhausted. Knowing that this will be my battle for the rest of my life makes my heart sink. One part of me wants to end the pain and suffering. Put a stop to the never-ending cycle of highs and lows and finally rest. The other part of me knows how far I have come and wants to fight. The reality, it would seem, is that I will never get "better". I see no end in sight and have no hope for any sort of catharsis.

I'm sure that in my depressed state I tend to think the worst, but I know that in a lot of ways, the pessimist in me is right. I have spent six years fighting the demons inside me, hoping that one day my shattered psyche could be at peace. This condition has nearly killed me on more than one occasion, and though I fought and won the battle, it is quite clear I am losing the war. I am trying so hard to stay positive and do the right thing. I do not want to be this way, think these things, and feel this pain, but this is the hand I have been dealt.

I'm just lost. I don't know what to do anymore. I can't go through this again. I don't have enough left in me to fight this. I fear the worst and try to hope for the best. Fucking BPD.

- XV

Revelations
September 22nd

The anxiety is only getting worse, and along with it comes an ever-deepening depression. My mind has often been my worst enemy in creating ridiculous scenarios that I obsess over and twist into a morbid conglomeration of bullshit. I do admire the creative capacity of the psyche, but I mostly curse it for sending me down a path of tachycardia and hyperhidrosis.

Recently I have had to do some serious thinking, made much harder by my mind's tendency to go WAY off the rails as mentioned above. There is a part of me that is starting to realize that despite how amazingly well things are going in my relationship, there have been things hiding just out of view that are slowly bubbling to the surface. Much of these bubbles contain paranoid thoughts born from my inclination to jump to conclusions and worst-case scenarios. However some bubbles contain realities that have the potential to blow up in my face.

I have always admired my girlfriend for her maturity and how well she has planned a future that can only be as bright as she is. There is a very good chance that much of this is in my head (I blame the BPD), but I know that to some extent, these things hold some truth. We are five years apart in age, and when I was that young, my life consisted of (besides all the pain and bullshit) partying, drugs, and having fun. I feel that in some way, I am holding her back from truly experiencing life as a college student.

I am at the point in my life where I have been through all of that and came out on the other side ready to move forward with my life. She has alluded to "missing the chance to be reckless and have fun", and it bothers me. Not because of the slightly sexual connotations (sewing her wild oats, as it were), but because if she, even in some small way, regrets that, then what else is she missing out on?

I know she is happy with me, and we love each other. However this is the age where she should be experimenting, partying, and enjoying life before entering the workforce and these activities becoming socially unacceptable. We are in two different phases of our lives, and trying to have a life together is sure to bring up some issues.

That in itself is not enough to cause a normal person anxiety, at least not to the extent that I feel. For me, it is as if my heart is about to explode. The thought of losing her because she is being 'held back' kills me. If she chose to pursue that part of her life, I would not hold it against her, but I would not be waiting to take her back when she has finished. It is ultimately her choice how to live her life. Mine has been by no means "normal", but I know

that sexual promiscuity and the party life is highly overrated –
and that is not for me to tell her.

I guess I just have a lot of thinking to do before I start this
conversation with her. I will need 100% honesty, no matter the
consequences. I cannot go on wondering if she regrets missing
out on those things. Wondering what she isn't telling me.

I know that with everything I am going through, this is the last
thing I need to stress about. It may seem silly, but it is not silly to
me. I know that if I lose her, I will backslide. That is not on her
though. I could be way off the mark in my thinking, but there
has been enough evidence for me to start asking these questions.

I have no idea how to proceed. I want to know the truth but I
am terrified of what the answer could be. As I write this entry,
my heart is going crazy in my chest. I feel sick and depressed. I
feel uncertainty and it is that feeling which is the hardest to bear.
Maybe I will get a moment of clarity and the answer will come to
me. For now, I suffer.

I told you my mind was my worst enemy.

- XV

Still Haunted
September 23rd

I came across my old external hard drive tonight. I had forgotten
all about it until I happened to come across it hiding in my
closet. As I looked through all the old pictures I had taken in the
brief time I thought I was a photographer, a picture of the bitch
who tore apart my life came up.

Normally I would get a little bitter and delete the picture. However in my emotionally weakened state it hit me harder than it should have. I never got any closure when she left, and the repercussions of what she did still, in some way, affect me to this day. I wish I was stronger, that I could just leave the past in the past. But the dirty whore called BPD makes that difficult. Or maybe I am just using BPD as a scapegoat. Who knows? Anyway, this is something easily fixed (temporarily) by a couple sedatives. Again, I did say my mind was my worst enemy (See above entry).

- XV

The Depravity of Old
September 24th

Continuing on from last night's post, the hard drive contained more than just a few pictures of the she-devil that nearly killed me. It also contained pictures of my arms cut to shreds, stitches holding the skin together. Pathetic ramblings much like my journals. Sad attempts at poetry, lamenting my shitty situation at the time. Even a sort of screenplay, where boredom clearly took hold and I had a very temporary aspiration to make a self-indulgent movie about my life.

In that script there was mostly truth, with a sort of M. Night Shyamalan-like twist at the end. Much of what was written reminded me of all the sick, depraved things I would do. It reminded me of my addiction to painkillers and how little I cared about my own well-being. Back then I was a shattered mess of a man. Except I was barely human, more of an abstraction of what one should look like. Most nights I would lay bloodied and high as a kite wishing I had the balls to end my misery.

I came close a few times. Hospitalizations punctuated with doctors and nurses telling me how lucky I was to have survived despite losing so much blood or taking so many pills. I sure as shit did not feel lucky. I just felt hopeless and lost. I was a failure in my eyes and a pathetic one at that. The self-pity led to self-mutilation to self-destruction. Looking back I am glad I did not 'finish the job', so to speak. It would have only hurt the ones I loved. It would have been a cowardly way out. Not that suicide is cowardly, but for me, I had options and help was offered. I was just too stubborn or scared to take what was offered. A coward.

I found a poem (and I use that word loosely) called "Bipolar Coaster". It was an immensely sarcastic response to being called that by a douche bag who was no prize himself. For how high I must have been to write it, I found it not too bad. It's not something I would share, but it is another reminder of the turbulent nightmare that was my life.

So why dwell? What do I get from looking back and reliving the pain that nearly cost me my life? Probably nothing but pain from opening old wounds that never healed properly. But through a lens of positivity, it shows me how far I have come. It almost seems like someone else wrote those words. It was a different time in what, to me, was a different life.

Maybe my masochism has not completely disappeared and looking at this sordid history brings on a familiar pain that, at one time, I would embrace (then numb with various pills). Pain used to define me. The physical type coming from my mysterious joint pain to the psychological pain that came out of nowhere and brought me to my knees.

For years my life was about chasing the high, numbing the pain, making myself bleed as punishment for whatever-the-fuck, and embracing the darkness that dwelled inside of me. So now comes the ultimate philosophical and existential question – Is that person, that thing, who was capable of all this sick depravity and self-destruction still inside me lying dormant, waiting for my guard to drop so it can once again take hold? I have no answer. No clue. With the downward spiral I seem to be in right now, how much more will it take to bring that horror back?

I would love to be optimistic, but it is quite hard to believe that this darkness has disappeared.

- XV

Unhinged
September 28th

I struggle on with the unrelenting depression and crippling anxiety. I still cannot uncover the reason why this decline began, or why it has continued. Out of nowhere the sickening feeling in my heart begins, making it hard to breathe. Then comes the shaking and sweaty palms. It is a horrible feedback loop where the seemingly idiopathic anxiety makes me anxious, compounding the feelings of uncertainty and impending doom.

It might sound overdramatic, but when the poisonous fog of depression rolls in, or the anxiety that has you struggling to catch a breath takes a hold of you, it is all that matters. What may seem utterly innocuous to one may be paralyzing to another. That is the hallmark of mental illness – it's subjectivity. In hundreds of pages spanning six years, I feel I have barely scratched the surface, for it is nearly impossible for one to understand just how debilitating these feelings can be.

At times, I feel that there is no reason to write these entries, no point in shouting in the dark to a crowd that will likely not hear me anyway. I suppose you can just add this feeling to the ever-rising pile of uncertainties that lie before me. Maybe no one will ever read these words, and maybe my goal of reducing stigma and helping people understand mental illness will go unfulfilled, but this remains an effective therapy for me. Self-care has never been my forte, but using these entries as a sort of valve to release the pressure that is the chaos in my mind remains beneficial to my psyche.

Ahead lies tough decisions and the proverbial crossroads. I can either fight for my well-being or I can roll over and accept the inevitable – this is for life. I want to fight. I want to be strong. I want to beat the hideous creature that is BPD. I also want to be realistic. Over the last six years I have lost so much. I am so fucking tired. So fucking drained. To think that once again I am in the midst of a battle for my psychological health is crushing, to say the least.

So much of me has been chipped and torn away over the years that I honestly don't know how much is left. I would love to look to my future with optimism, and look to my past as a lesson well-learned. I would love to say that I came out from the living Hell that was my life in one piece, so I can do it again. I want to say that I have learned valuable lessons that will help me weather another storm…

But the purpose of this is to be truthful.

- XV

Fighting Demons
September 29th

"I self-destruct, silence of the anger
And I laughed alone
I feel like a fool,
Like a mad man fighting demons
Pigs and effigies
I feel my abuse, a drug addled nothing
I understand him"

- Where the Angels Burn – William Control

A common theme for me has been fighting the demons that seem to have taken up permanent residence inside of me (or a long-term lease, at the very least). At first I resisted them, but |I was not strong enough to hold them at bay. Eventually, after I was worn down, I began to accept the demons. I embraced them as part of a dichotomy that made me who I was. Light and dark, good and evil. Embracing them only lead me down a path of drug-fueled benders and shattered relationships.

After a few years, I slowly learned that while it is okay to acknowledge these demons, embracing them can only end in pain and misery. I was certain that they had no part to play in a healthy life, and once again I pushed them down. I feel that lately, along with my psychological deterioration, they have been clawing at my insides, fighting to be let out.

So what the fuck do I do? I have proven moderation is not one of my strengths. Do I mark off a day each month to appeal to these beasts and their aberrant desires? One day where I let loose the very thing that took over and destroyed me before? Obviously continuing to repress them has been tasking and potentially detrimental to my mental health.

Fuck, I have no idea. I swing like the proverbial pendulum, back and forth, from uncertainty to worse uncertainty. My indecisiveness causes me so much stress that I get random panic attacks. Like I said before, it is an endless feedback loop, where the fact that I am depressed will depress me more and the fact that I am anxious causes me even more anxiety. I cannot, for the life of me, seem to win.

Anyway, all that bullshit aside, let me complain about something different before I wrap this woefully pathetic and confusing lament up. I feel like I am going to be sick. It could be the alcohol and pills mixing (no, not in dangerous doses so simmer down). For the last little while I have been coming home and downing a few (or so) drinks. I am not notorious for handling my stress well, and numbing with substance is a common solution for me.

My irritability is also getting worse, and my girlfriend is seeing a side of me that I wished she would never see. I don't get mad, I just get quiet and short with her. I don't want to push her away. I hope she understands.

- XV

Marathon
September 30th

"The mind is its own place, and in itself can make a heaven of hell, a hell of heaven."

- Paradise Lost – John Milton

I saw my doctor today. I moved my appointment up a month because I knew I could not wait until the end of October to see him. After sitting in the waiting room for an hour and a half (he's usually on time), fidgeting nervously and shaking from the anxiety, my name was called.

In the room I probably looked like I was tweaking by the way I looked. By now he is used to seeing me in pretty rough shape. After telling him the truth about how poorly I was doing, he agreed that my case was out of his element. I am waiting on a call to see if his referral to a psychiatrist was successful or not. He seemed to think the sooner, the better. He also increased my clonazepam dose from 'as needed' to three times daily. Twenty pills lasted me all of last month (up to today). He now has given me NINETY pills for the next thirty days.

I don't want to take that much. I understand the necessity of it, but I do not want to fall back into old habits, using substance as a crutch. I may start with two a day and see how I do. I hadn't experienced a panic attack in well over a year, maybe more. Now I have had about three a week for the last month or so.

I feel like I have been running a marathon. One that lasts six years and involves running to doctor after doctor, from medication to medication, from addiction to addiction, and diagnosis to diagnosis. I am tired. I have said this a million times already, but I can feel the exhaustion setting in. With everything going on at home, pushing myself too hard at work, and putting school off AGAIN, it's no wonder I am crumbling.

- XV

Breaking Point
October 4th

With everything in my life being so turbulent and all-around shitty, my relationship keeps me going. I was recently faced with a harsh reality – I may fuck that up too. She has been amazing, standing by me through my mood swings, irritability, and anxiety. Last night was hard. She told me that I was an asshole sometimes, and she was tired of it. It was a small thing that set it off, but this has obviously been building up for a while.

For the first time, I saw evidence that there is something wrong in our relationship. I have been so caught up in my decline and my depression that I forgot she is there for me. I don't want to push her away because she means the world to me. She keeps me centred amidst the chaos and the bullshit. It is no secret to those that know me that I can be an asshole, but when she told me I was one last night, it devastated me. I never meant to treat her that way, and I cannot use my BPD as a crutch all the time. It plays a huge part in my mood and how I act, but when it comes down to it, I am responsible for my own words and actions.

I think we sorted things out with her agreeing to be more open and let me know when things bother her, and me being more careful about how I treat her.

I slipped and bought more Percocet last week. I can rationalize it all I want by saying that I need to be numbed; that the constant bombardment of anxiety and depression is getting to me so much I can't take it anymore, but I know it's not good for me. I told my girlfriend I had been taking them and she was understandably upset and worried. Looking at my bedside table, four pill bottles sit in a line. Those four different medications I take daily, as they are prescribed to me. I can't imagine what those are doing to my body, so what is the big deal over some perks?

My mind is a mess right now. Even this entry is jumbled and confusing. Maybe I will try again when I have time to sort out the mess in my mind.

- XV

On This Day in 2012...
October 6th

Here is an entry from one of my hand-written journals dating back to October 6th, 2012. I feel this is a good choice as it directly relates to the reason I have written countless entries spanning almost six years. This is exactly as it is in the journal – with no omissions or editing, as always.

"Reading over the three journals I have so far truly gives me perspective on my sickness. A major theme seems to be destruction, both self-destruction and destroying those close to me. I have left a smoldering trail of wreckage, scars that will never heal. People I once loved, maybe still do, see me for what I am. Damaged and damaging.

I have literally put my blood into these journals. Writing post after post, not really knowing why. Maybe I need to empty my head, maybe I think one day someone will read this and understand, or maybe there isn't a reason. Maybe I just write for the sake of writing. All I know is that I have created a written record of my collapse, and ultimately, my demise.

With everything piling up on top of me, it's getting more and more difficult to face life, to want life, and not take my life. I'm hoping that tearing off the mask I wear, I will have one less thing pushing me down.

There is one person I seem to have trouble letting go of. In fact, we are texting right now for the first time in a while. I hurt her, pushed her away, and still haven't been able to forgive myself for losing her. It makes me sick to my stomach knowing I fucked up and will never have what we had again. I live every day with regret; alone and in pain. Frankly it's <u>exactly</u> what I deserve. I am not human. I am not meant to succeed, be happy, or be healthy. I've accepted that. Knowing where to go from here is impossible. I'm stuck. Going nowhere, doing nothing."

Hmm. I like to think a lot has changed since I wrote that entry, drowning in self-loathing and regret. However some things remain unchanged. I retain my pessimistic mindset, but not to the degree it was in 2012. Relationships always ended in pain for me, and I never realized the iron grip they had on my soul. I spent so many months, even years, caught up in an idea; what a relationship should be. I was so clouded by this I did not realize that it was not meant to be.

I have always been of the mind that people never change, that despite changes in their behaviour, they are fundamentally the same. Reading over old journals feels like reading someone else's story. The fact that I do not remember writing those does not surprise me, but the fact that it seems so long ago, in a different life as a different person, does. I am proud of the changes I have made since then. The very challenge of ever recovering from such horrific events and such brutal pain seemed insurmountable. I am not, and likely will never be, free from the haunted past. Reminders of who or what I was are everywhere, and letting go is the hardest thing I have ever had to do. I hate dwelling, I hate obsessing, but those times are as much a part of me as the happier times I have experienced recently.

I guess the moral of the story is that nothing but death is permanent. Life changes, for the better or for worse, but you always have a choice. You can always decide how you let challenges affect you, and in the end, that (to me) is the measure of who you are.

- XV

A Day in the Life
October 7th

I wake up feeling groggy and disoriented, hungover from the handful of sleepers it takes to knock me out each night. I glare at my alarm, thinking 'Already?". It feels like I have only slept a few hours, tops. On my bedside table sits four, sometimes five pill bottles. Each has its own purpose. The one I reach for is my antidepressant. Two each morning. Sometimes, if I am lucky enough to have some, I will chase them down with three or four Percocet.

My daily routine never really changes. I struggle to get out of bed and get ready for work at 8 a.m. each day (except weekends). I am barely conscious as I make my way in, and already the anxiety is kicking in as the thoughts race through my head. What bullshit is waiting for me at work? Who will stress me out? Will I have an anxiety attack? Can I make it through the day? Will I finally snap?

Work is a blur as I go about my routine, only half present. I feel like everyone notices that something is off about me; that they can see through the mask I put on every day. Clonazepam time. It's easier that way. Flying under the radar soothes my anxiety (only slightly) and ensures that no one catches on to just how detached I am. It is tiresome wearing that mask. It means that you are doing it to hide, to make others happy, to push down the crushing depression and anxiety.

I constantly watch the clock, which has this funny way of running backwards at times. I am good at what I do. I am proud of much of my work, but in my current state, I really don't give a shit anymore. Quitting time has me catching the bus home, another stressful endeavour. I feel people looking at me and I wonder what they see. I wonder if they can see the pain in my eyes or the shaking of my hands. I know it is not rational, but nothing that goes on in my mind is.

At home there is a brief sense of relief – I made it another day. I pop open a beer, and my night of isolating myself in my bedroom begins, where one beer turns into seven and minutes turn to hours. Clonazepam time. So I write. Or I watch Netflix. Or I just lay in my bed and listen to music, trying to forget the pain I feel. Sometimes, if I am "lucky" I will have some pills to numb my body and mind.

When I am too tired or bored of all that, I attempt sleep. One Trazodone, one Mirtazapine, and sometimes two Clonazepam – my nighttime cocktail designed to put me to sleep, however with only 50% efficiency.

Rinse. Repeat. Again. And again. And again.

Clonazepam time.

- XV

Hostility
October 12th

Most of the time I feel angry and irritable. I snap at people for little things and I can't figure out why. I know that this isn't me; I feel different. When I get in that kind of mood I cannot control myself even though I am fully aware of how I am acting. Something is wrong and I am afraid of pushing people away by being an asshole.

My hope is that this new psychiatrist can figure this out for me. Until I see him in two weeks, I will have to deal with this the best I can. I hate being this way. It feels like there is acid in my veins and it is more than just irritability. It is much deeper. It is, at times, pure anger and even hatred. I can't go on like this for much longer. Everything seems to be falling apart and I feel like I have been eviscerated and am pointlessly struggling to keep my guts inside my body. Or something shitty like that.

- XV

Over the Edge
October 13th

It's just one thing after another, and a whole lot of the same old bullshit. On top of the general anger and misery of late, there is a mounting anxiety that threatens to incapacitate me.

I took my driver's test again today as I had let my license expire four years ago. It wasn't even the road test, just the written part. I barely made it through as the shaky tendrils of anxiety clenched my throat. Clonazepam time. I passed, but it was another reminder that I am not okay. Right after I learned that I do in fact have to wait a year until I can take my road test and be able

91

to drive alone. Fuck sakes! I was told I wouldn't have to. Such is my life right now.

After another anxiety-fueled trip to the grocery store I come home to my mother and brother fighting and my aunt in tears. I am getting to the point where I simply cannot handle this stress anymore. I can feel it eating away at me, breaking me apart piece by piece. Clonazepam time.

I feel weak, uneasy, afraid, angry, and hateful. I am becoming something horrible as I lose the fight against the emotional bombardment I am receiving. I can't do this much longer. The meds barely take the edge off and who the fuck knows what else this is doing to my body and my already battered and bruised mind.

It will not take much to push me over the edge at this point.

- XV

Crushed
October 14th

I'll start off with the good news – I got the job I applied for. It's the same one I am doing now, but with a longer contract. The interview made me anxious and I barely made it through, but I guess it was enough to impress the interviewers.

Now to the shitty stuff. I know that I can sometimes become so absorbed in my own misery and stress that I fail to 'see the forest for the trees'. I get distracted by my own issues that I become blind to other people's issues. Unfortunately, the one person I am hurting the most is the one I love the most. She told me tonight that I never make an effort to see her, that she makes all the sacrifices and changes her schedule to suit mine, and that she doesn't get how I don't realize when I am acting like a dick when I am feeling low. I do realize it, and it kills me. This whole thing does. I can't lose her.

She blames herself for some of it; her own insecurities can play mind games on her, and I get that. But unless she tells me when things bother her, instead of waiting for me to ask and pouring out a few months' worth of issues, I cannot work to fix this. I hate myself for how I have been acting. I do not like who I am becoming. I can't lose her.

- XV

Dark Thoughts
October 15th

As before, along with my declining mood, comes the return of the dark thoughts. I blamed my own Dark Passenger, as I have journaled about before, for these; as if it took away my culpability in the matter. We all have dark thoughts. Most are fleeting, such as when someone cuts you off while you are driving. Maybe you think of pulling the guy from his car and beating the piss out of him. Quickly, the thought is gone, and you go on with your day. Rarely do you obsess about it for days, even weeks. That seems to be my struggle.

I have battled the darkest parts of my psyche, then embraced them. I have seen the reality – in us exists a dichotomy that defines us as human. A light vs. dark battle waged each and every day in each and every person. There are those select few who live in denial. I think it's more about fear. It is socially unacceptable to beat the piss out of a shitty driver, but is it really immoral to have those thoughts? They seem so automatic, so engrained in our nature that even the idea that someone could live without darkness is absurd.

I am not proposing anarchy, I am simply stating a truth. For the most part, the dark part of your being should not be displayed in public. But I do argue that exploration of that side of your being is just as important as that of your good side. I went years questioning why these thoughts occurred, why I sometimes acted on them (usually at the expense of my own health), and why I seemed to be plagued more than others. It was a while before I realized that it is simply human nature, and the measure of who you are is based on how you act upon the light or the dark.

I digress. With my recent shitty mood has come a 'dark renaissance' of sorts. The thoughts came, strolling casually across my mind at first. Now they seem to be gallivanting across like some sort of fucking dance ensemble. I guess when the psyche is weakened, you are more prone to these types of things. I have to admit that they bother me a great deal. I obsess, question, and worry about what it all means – an existential crisis built upon a slip in mental health.

Unlike before, I will face these thoughts head-on, knowing that in reality, they have no power. I know there is good inside me, maybe in equal parts. With depression comes self-defeating thinking, obsessions (in some cases), and an inclination to explore the darker aspects of who you are. But I can handle it. Right?

- XV

Lost My Way
October 20th

I was on a path to wellness; confidently walking towards a goal
where I would finally be happy and do something meaningful
with my life. After 5 year-old charges cut apart any chance of
continuing in my studies, a chain-reaction started. Since then, the
oft-mentioned decline has been in motion.

At the time it did not seem that devastating. I knew it was
bullshit and I was mad. Very mad. At the bitch that ruined my
life, at the people who told me it would be no problem to pursue
this career with a record, and at myself for thinking that I was
out of the woods. Gradually I began noticing that I was slipping
away from the positive path I had been on. The dark thoughts,
the emptiness, and the unrelenting depression came back.

So here I am, eight months later, trying to find a reason to look
on the bright side. I look and all I see is a foggy haze that
obscures any potential motivation to be optimistic. The pain I
feel is reminiscent of those dark years, when all I did was
consume drugs, break hearts, isolate, and self-destruct. It is a
heavy feeling in my chest, yet the echoes of the pain suggest a
profound emptiness.

Nothing excites me. Nothing motivates me. My future looks
twisted, uncertain, and abstract, leaving me wondering what I am
working toward. I can't go to school because I need to work to
make money, I can't get a decent job without school, I don't
know how the fuck my relationship is going to work when she
goes off to another school in another town, and I feel like I will
have gone completely insane before any of this has a chance to
play out. Fuck…

- XV

Bipolar?
October 27th

My new psychiatrist seems to be leaning towards a diagnosis of bipolar disorder. That would certainly throw a damper on the title of these journals, but it also has more profound implications. Getting my diagnosis of BPD meant I finally had a name to put to the pain I was feeling. It meant that the prognosis could be good, and for a while it was. Now yet another diagnosis has been thrown at me, causing me to rethink everything I know about myself and my illness.

If this diagnosis is accurate, then I am faced with a different prognosis. When I am manic, I have depression to look forward to, and when I am depressed, mania is not too far off. The silver lining is that maybe now I can receive more targeted treatment that will be more effective.

Other than that I have been battling bronchitis and losing, for the most part. It sucks serious ass and I have had little energy to do anything. I still feel like I am cracking up and falling apart, but what's new?

- XV

Pitch Black
November 1st

I am utterly and completely depressed. The depth of it is unlike anything I have experienced before. Life feels void of pleasure or joy. Hope has vanished and I am left in a swirling vortex of pain and misery. I am scared of what will happen in this continues. It is too much to bear and it is bringing me closer and closer to the point of insanity. I really fucking hope my new psychiatrist has some real answer for me tomorrow.

This is bad. And when I say it is really, really bad, I mean it is fucking cataclysmic.

- XV

Decay
November 5th

I can't eat. I can't sleep. I can barely get through the day anymore. These new medications are not helping me sleep and they are making me into a zombie. I have no affect, no personality, and no energy. On top of that, getting off my antidepressant and sleeping pills is hard on my body.

I guess I forgot to mention that my new psychiatrist confirmed bipolar disorder as my new diagnosis, not only changing how I see myself but the title of this journal *(exeunt BPD, enter BD)*. More importantly it means a new type of medication (mood stabilizers) can be used and will hopefully be more effective than those I have tried in the past.

The point of all of these journals remains the same. What mental illness you are suffering from is irrelevant (for this purpose). I am suffering, and if these can bring understanding, knowledge, insight, empathy, and even hope into someone's life, I will be happy. Odds are, this will not happen. I don't even know what the fuck I am doing anymore.

I am failing my ONE class, which is online, my performance at work is suffering, my relationship is suffering, and I feel like every day makes it harder to climb out of this hole. I am falling apart.

- XV

Medication Overload
November 9th

I have great respect for my new psychiatrist. He knows what he is doing, he is figuring out what many doctors before couldn't, and he is determined to find the right medications to treat me. The issue I have is how many meds I am on now, and how much I have to take. Here is my daily pill routine:

* Wake up, 300mg bupropion
* Throughout the day, 0.5mg clonazepam (as needed)
* Before bed, 750mg divalproex, 6mg Abilify, 5mg escitalopram, and 1mg clonazepam

So, that is 2 pills in the morning, one through the day, and NINE at night for a whopping total of TWELVE pills each day. I am having a bit of trouble keeping track of these, and though it does seem overwhelming, I trust this doctor. He wants to find the right combination; a process that is just as much medicine as art.

The side-effects have been pretty bad, ranging from neck pain to insomnia, diarrhea to irritability, and headaches to muscle pain/ stiffness (and a noticeable lack of stiffness elsewhere). I need to give these a chance to work, so I will soldier through the pain and hope that finally, after 6 years I have found the right drug combination to compliment the amazing counselling I am getting. My counsellor has gone over and above what is expected, and it helps more than I can express.

There are very mixed emotions going on in my head, as well as several manic thoughts bouncing around. My life has a theme of chaos and uncertainty right now, but it all seems much more manageable with my amazing girlfriend who has been incredible through all of my mood swings and bullshit. I could not ask for a better person to love and to love me. In just under two weeks, we will have been together for a YEAR! For me, that is unbelievable. She makes all of this more bearable.

- XV

"Bipolar Coaster"
November 10th

I may have mentioned this before, but about 6 years ago I was dubbed (by some douche bag) a "bipolar coaster". How strange that, after all these years, he was right! This douche bag saw in me a pattern, and though the title was likely a product of his inherent doucheness, his accuracy surpassed that of countless doctors and counsellors.

Nostalgia aside, I am still not completely sold on this diagnosis. I never have been on any diagnosis for that matter. BPD always made the most sense, however it still felt like a pair of slacks too tight in the groin.

My symptoms seem to be increasing exponentially (see previous post), and it is difficult to determine what is a result of the medications and what is borne of my illness. My emotions are in a state of rapid and aggressive flux, while at the same time I feel flat. I guess the mania comes and goes more often than before, but it coincides with the medication change. It makes no sense that my treatment would exacerbate my condition.

I must be patient and give the meds time to work, but the insomnia and constant emotional fluctuations are getting exhausting and irritating. I can't focus. I'm unsteady. I feel like I am in the throes of a nose-dive and the controls are damaged. Even now I am having trouble focusing on this entry and staying on a single topic. Maybe that's my cue to sign off if I can't even stay on.......

- XV

So...Fucking...Tired
November 11th

I can barely move. Work is torture. Even going up stairs is exhausting. I have lost another 2 pounds and am falling deeper into this... whatever-the-fuck. I grow tired of the same old song played over and over, as if it were the only song in the world. A sorrowful lament called 'Pain'.

Fuck it, fuck that song, fuck this pain, fuck this diagnosis, fuck this insomnia, and fuck this same old shit. I'm tired of it.

- XV

Like Looking Into the Past
November 15th

A friend of mine is hospitalized for mental health issues. What she is going through seems similar to where I was at her age, about three years ago. She confided in me knowing my history; knowing I would not judge her or call her weak. Things seem dark right now but I do believe that she can beat this.

If there is a silver lining to the hell I went through over the last six years, it is that now I am better equipped to help those in need and those in similar situations. Even though I am having a hard time adjusting to the new diagnosis, new meds, lack of sleep, lack of appetite, and so on, I can still pick someone up who has fallen and hopefully help them see past the fog to a future where they have defeated the ugly creature that is (in her case) BPD.

I am still not 100% sold on my new diagnosis, but the meds seem to be starting to work (save for a few unpleasant side-effects). As always, I will trudge through the shit and the piss in search of the answer to the age old question, "How can I finally be happy?"

- XV

3-North-C
November 18th

I don't know what the point is anymore. Typing away day after day; and for what? A few close friends to read my misery and thoughts? The irony of writing this post is even bothering me.

Anyway I visited my friend who finally made it onto the inpatient floor (3 North C) of the hospital. I have been there multiple times and things have changed, though some things have not. I found myself envying her for being there, as if I wanted to be committed and in her shoes. As if I wanted a break from the horrifically repetitive routine of my life and take some time off.

Now don't get me wrong, it is no vacation to be in there, but she seemed better. Something about it made me want to be there too.

Maybe I am just losing my mind (even more). I am happy to see her doing better and that I can help, but sometimes, it gets tiring being the caretaker and not the patient.

- XV

Weight of Regret
November 19th

"Forgive and forget,
It's just a memory
It won't get me very far this time
Is what I've done to you unforgivable?
Silence fills the room
And I get the message.
Emptiness is all that's left this time.
Is what I meant to you that forgettable?"

- Just a Taste – Scary Kids Scaring Kids

I spent years suffering from the weight of the pain I felt at losing the girl I thought I loved, and who I thought loved me. She simply laid the charges on me and walked away. No message. No phone call, nothing. I was left with no closure and no answers, the worst combination for a masochistic drug addict.

Why am I reaching this far back into my life? To me, this is still going on. The ripple-effect from the charges not only caused years of self-harm, repeated overdoses, and misery – it had an impact on my life as a whole. I am far less trusting, more cynical, I was kicked out of the nursing program nearly a year ago, and I STILL cannot get a pardon until July 2019.

I am told over and over not to dwell on the past, but it is so fucking hard to let go and forget years of pain – years of being drugged up alone, making cut after cut all over my body, hating myself, blaming myself for what happened to her and the others I destroyed after, and losing every friend I had (except one).

 I guess right now I am just fucking miserable and so these thoughts come easier to me. Tomorrow is my one year anniversary with M, and I couldn't be happier to be with her. That doesn't mean that the weight of my past is gone. It remains, and will for the rest of my life. The past is what makes you who you are, right? But you also can't let your past define who you are. MAKE UP YOUR FUCKING MINDS!.

- XV

Defeated
November 22nd

I feel defeated. Utterly defeated. Yesterday I had a slight breakdown/existential crisis with my girlfriend. I was so depressed it hurt. I told her how I felt like I was spinning my wheels, as in doing all this work and making all these changes, only end up in the same puddle of shit and piss. Six years and my diagnosis has ONCE AGAIN changed, I take 13 pills a day (exactly as he prescribed), I go see my counsellor weekly, and I no longer cut or use drugs to numb the pain.

So where am I? Twenty-five years old and living in my mother's basement, stuck in second year of a program I should have finished three years ago, the future is foggy, I'm a mess, my meds are causing shitty side-effects, and I feel like I am losing the battle for my mental health. As I said before: spinning my fucking wheels. On a positive note, I have an amazing girlfriend and a good job (even if it seems like I will be stuck there forever).

I guess I just wanted my life to be more than it is at this age. It is wearing on me and I do not feel strong enough to keep fighting. I am falling apart and I don't know what is going to happen if/when I finally snap.

- XV

Eat My Dust! (Life Said)
November 23rd

Fuck... Just fuck. I wake up too early, exhausted, sore, weight dropped even more, and miserable. To top it off, if I don't pay my school $680 soon they will de-register me from a course that I can barely keep up with. Yes, 'A' course. One. Singular. Motivation has gone out the window and floated off like the proverbial plastic bag in the wind. Out of reach as it dances along the currents.

I just don't know what to do anymore. I'm so fucking lost. How can I get my shit together and get back on track? Seriously, not a rhetorical question. Anyone?

- XV

Eternal Unrest
November 25th

Am I in complete denial, fighting for something unobtainable? Is the thought of a normal life where I am happy possible? I doubt it more and more every day. I am SO fucking tired of switching from diagnosis to diagnosis, medication to medication, and highs to lows. I'm so close to being just fucking done. I've said it before: for me, there will likely be no catharsis, no release, and no absolution for the sins of my past and present. Call me cynical, but how long can a man go being battered and beaten by an invisible entity? Being constantly bombarded by one negative emotion after another wears on you, especially when your body and soul is already bruised and broken?

Negative, negative, negative. Negativity comes naturally to me. Can you blame me for being all piss and vinegar because of a life that took a horrible turn six years ago? I have never (and will never) be the same. Why couldn't I just fucking finish Queen's and get my degree? Why did all this bullshit have to happen? Those questions will never be answered, so all I can do is deal with the shit hand I have been dealt as well as I can. And I have, as long as I can. I am cracking again. I can feel it. The thing is, I am not worried. I am just done.

This is not a final entry, a cry for help, nor is it a suicide note. It is an admission of defeat and an acceptance of a life that will never have stability again. I am mentally ill. I have to deal with it, or don't. Look where not dealing with it got me before – numb from the drugs and in the hospital more times than I can remember.

So now I have to think of what I can do. I can look forward with an empty soul and trudge on through the barren wasteland. I can fight harder than ever in the vain hope that THIS time I will figure myself out (not fucking likely). Or I can give up, give in, and take myself out. The latter will not happen. Been there, tried that, got the scars to remember it by. So the first option is what I will do.

I do not know where this twisted path will take me, or if there is a higher reason I do not yet understand for all my pain and suffering. Whatever the case, I will walk forward, wearing the mask everyone wants to see, while underneath I am empty and broken; a hollow shell with just a flicker of life left inside created by Her. She is the reason I keep walking. Otherwise, sadly, I see no point. Call me pathetic, but six years is a long time to live in sorrow.

- XV

Instability & Chaos
November 26th

How do I follow that last entry? What's left to say? My new approach of losing hope and not caring about a future where I am happy will have implications, but I don't care, remember? I don't know what the fuck to do anymore. Like I said before, I am tired of the same old story – shitty symptoms, diagnosis, medications, more shitty symptoms, new diagnosis, etc. How am I supposed to hold hope when the chaos in my head and life are driving me crazier than whatever the underlying psychopathology is?

My girlfriend doesn't understand, and I do not blame her. She didn't sign up for this and obviously has no experience with this shit. What is she supposed to do but sit and watch as I deteriorate, falling into the familiar pit of emptiness and despair. I hate this. I cannot go through this again. I just can't.

I am not strong enough.

- XV

Dormancy Makes the Mind Go Wander
November 27th

It's Friday night and I am sitting in my room alone. That, for me, is a dangerous thing. Alone with my thoughts is a scary place that I normally would not want to go. However, since my new "no fucks given" attitude has taken over, I (inherently) give no fucks!

My mind wanders to thoughts of the stinging release of the slice of a knife. To the numbing brilliance of an opiate-fueled haze. To dwelling on how alone and miserable I really am. This is a recipe for disaster. Or for a night where I get numb and take my mind off all the bullshit that swirls around me like leaves in the wind. Maybe it isn't such a bad idea...

- XV

Addendum: Or maybe it is...

Undertow
November 29th

Keeping my head above water is a constant struggle that is only growing more tasking by the day. I am all over the place. I can't focus. I am disorganized and forgetful; tired and weak. I haven't been this skinny since the days of my cocaine addiction and I am worried that all of this will start destroying my fragile psyche piece by piece.

It is too late for optimism or sunny outlooks. I can only move forward and take shit as it comes. The days when I would numb this pain out has caused this to feel so much worse now. Facing the stark reality that without the drugs I am this weak hits hard. Not that the drugs made me strong, but how much could shit affect me if I am flying high or numbed out?

I don't know what to do. I just don't. Fuck.

- XV

Still Trying to Find My Way
December 1st

For years I have searched for who I really am. Every time I think I have it figured out, the cruel hand of life bitch-slaps me with the reality that I simply do not know. Everything is so skewed and abstract that clarity is an impossibility, forever out of my reach. I drive myself insane with trying to understand what is going on in my head; trying to put order to the chaos. It only serves to drive me mad.

I cannot articulate the way I am feeling right now. Here is my attempt: It is like I am sinking further down into a pit and can no longer see the circle of light at the top. Escape is more impossible with every inch I sink down into the dark abyss of my mind. The pit is filled with the bitter taste of hate and resentment; clouds of poisonous depression linger and I am up to my knees in shit, piss, and vinegar. The walls leak sorrow and disgust, threatening to fall in on me at any moment now. The emptiness I feel inside only lends more space to the overwhelming despair and hopelessness growing inside me like some kind of fucking malignant tumor.

I hate myself for the things I have done, for the sins of my past and present. I hate myself for the things I think and say. This toxic self-hatred fuels the fire of my downfall as it leeches what little life from my body I have left. The scars covering my body and the cracks where I was haphazardly put back together threaten to tear open and spill blood until I am left as empty as I feel. I feel guilty for the people I have hurt, the people I am hurting, and the people I will hurt. The guilt of my own self-absorption in my disease is eating away at me, and even though I know it will only worsen my circumstance, I still push away those few who care and try to help me.

Maybe I feel like I do not deserve it. Maybe I feel like what I do now cannot possibly erase the crimes of my past. I am forever damned to a life where I am lost, unable to feel fulfilled and happy, where wellness will only be a dream and only a dream.

This is my pity-party, and you are all invited. But how much of this is wrong? To me, it is all truth, but to you it may seem like the desperate ramblings of a sad, broken (and somewhat twisted) man filled with bitterness and self-loathing. Maybe we are both right. Pain is subjective. What may feel like a stubbed toe to you can feel like I just had my arms cut off.

She is the reason I hold on, fight, and look to the future. She is what holds me together. All I know is how I feel. All I know is that this is destroying me. I cannot go on like this. I need answers. Fast.

- XV

Is It Time?
December 2nd

Is it time that I wrap this set of journals up? Move on and cut the cord tying me to these countless pages of misery and unanswered questions? I honestly do not know what my end game really is. Release another book to be as ignored and undiscovered as the first one? Maybe. I will always need something that empties my head, so as long as my head is full of chaos and misery, I will have these pages.

The big question is what am I trying to accomplish here? On a personal note, I need to empty my head and sort my thoughts out. Release the pressure valve and let off some steam, as it were. For the big picture, maybe I can help someone who suffers as I do. Maybe I can bring about understanding of mental illness and speak for those that have no voice or unable to articulate the pain they feel into words. I do not want to be an international best-seller, I want my work to make a difference – that way I know my suffering wasn't all for nothing.

I just need to find a purpose, a direction in my life to start walking toward, free of the burden that accompanies my condition. I am a work in progress, with A LOT of work still to be done. I have hit some 'snags' to say the least, but despite all the punches to the groin and stabs into my heart, I somehow continue to stumble through life.

Somehow. This mask I wear to appease people is slipping more and more, and people are noticing. I am pale, skinny, and look like a bag of shit that was shit on by another bag of shit that had consumed shit the day before. I feel it in my tattered heart and in my weak bones that I am nearing the end of my rope – walking along the edge of a cliff, slowly inching towards the edge. NO! Of course I am not suicidal. If I was, I would have done it. I have her to live for; my family and (though this is becoming a weaker reason) myself to fight for.

The aforementioned cliff leads to drop where there is no bottom, only an eternal descent with some well-placed rocks along the way to smack against on your way down. It isn't just my stumbling through life that is getting me closer to the edge. I feel it pulling, as if gravity has doomed me as well.

Yes. This volume of my life is nearly complete. It will be done when it is done, but I feel a profound change coming. For better? For worse? I do not know. But it looms in the distance, blurred by the proverbial poisonous cloud that surrounds me.

- XV

Rebuilding
December 3rd

When the shit-storm started, I was slowly broken down into tiny pieces. I rebuilt, however I would never be complete again. I feel like I am falling apart again. I'm tearing at the seams and the foundation crumbles. Maybe I need to fall apart again. Maybe it will give me a chance to rebuild into a better me once again.

The only issue is that, once again, I will lose parts of myself forever. The act of falling apart has risks in itself. There is no guarantee I can rebuild again and no way of knowing if I will be rebuilt any better than I am now.

There is something fundamentally wrong, and the worst part is having no answers. I saw my psychiatrist today to no avail. He asked me the same series of questions. I struggled to answer, because with him it seems like there is a right and wrong answer, even though it's just about how I feel. In fact, at one point he asked me to give another example of my irritability because, and I quote, "That example doesn't really fit here." What the fuck? Give me some multiple choice questions then so I know what the fuck to say!

I just need to have faith that this is a means to an end – a good end. As for now, it seems like he isn't clear on what is going on with me. I am all over the place and he seems to simply be doing damage control by fighting the symptoms as they come. I guess I need to stabilize before he looks at the bigger picture, but how long will that take? I'm growing tired of this, and even more tired of the way he tosses meds at me like some old guy feeding birds bread by the handful.

TRY THIS! No? Hmm. This? No?! Hmmmmm. Maybe this one? (et cetera). He has given me two new meds for a total of seven. Yes folks, fucking SEVEN! One of them is an antidepressant that, six years ago, gave me a psychotic break. So if there is a large gap between posts, his little plan did not go as expected. He knows about the adverse reaction, but I guess he figures the reward outweighs the risk.

He told me to trust him, to take the meds as prescribed, and to listen to his advice and be patient. I agreed. I will, at whatever cost. If this sorts my shit out, lay it on me, Doc.

- XV

What The Pain is All For
December 4th

I look back on my life and wonder, what is all of this for? What am I working towards? I ask myself this question every so often, but I will go into more detail, open old wounds so you can better understand me, and of course – censor nothing.

She was beautiful, in the innocent and cute way. Which was awfully deceiving because I sometimes sensed there was something much darker underneath. I was a stickler for a pretty face and her romantic view of us. I finally felt good about myself and I looked forward and saw a future. After dropping out of university in 2009 due to worsening depression her and I still saw each other, though things had been rocky.

She saw me about a week and a half before Christmas wearing a hospital bracelet. She was quiet and withdrawn. After asking over and over again, she finally told me why – she was dying. Her Kidneys were failing and causing other issues that made her terminal. In retrospect, it was a story full of holes and bullshit, but at the time it meant I was going to lose her. I couldn't see past my own misery and heart-break to the logic that would tear her story apart. Maybe I didn't want to.

The next week was spent with her talking of death, of taking it into her own hands, and of being free for the first time. I was horrified. She said if I told anyone, she would do it anyways and die alone. I could not keep this to myself so I reached out to her sister, who called me a liar and said her sister would never do that. I was stuck. Falling deeper into my own suffering, I mentally could not take on hers, too.

On December 21st, 2009 she picked me up from a friend's house. She was quiet and focused and I immediately knew there was something wrong. She was going to kill herself that day, the darkest night of the year, in her typical poetic style. What do I say? What do I do? Can I stop her? Would she just do it anyway the next chance she got? Should she die alone? The battle roared in my head between better judgement, empathy, and helplessness. We drove – fast – down the icy road towards her place. I begged her to slow down, but she was determined. I begged her not to end her life, but she was determined. She suddenly pulled over and ran to her truck, grabbing a bottle of washer fluid, threatening to drink it. NO! I yelled, You will just throw it up and burn yourself. Please! She reluctantly put it back into the trunk and we carried don, tears in our eyes.

She pulled into her house and grabbed three bottles of Tylenol #2's she had been stashing away. She got back in the car and I looked at her, then the bottles, and told her it wouldn't work. When she asked why, I for some reason I will never understand, told her milk coats the stomach so you are less likely to throw up when taking an overdose. She quickly went in a grabbed some milk.

We drove around until it was dark and the snow was falling lightly overhead. She pulled the car into a turnaround area near a forest that we used to go to. She shut the car off, got out, and we started walking. She had been slowly and methodically popping pills and chasing it with milk for over an hour. She suddenly stopped and tilted her head back, letting the snow fall on her white skin, maybe for the last time. She rolled up her sleeves and I remember the faint moonlight peeking through the clouds made her seem as though she was glowing. I felt like I was in a nightmare, like what was happening was not real and I would wake up in my bed sweating as I had been lately.

She started crying and we hugged, standing there for 10 seconds or 10 minutes. As she pulled back from the hug, she apologized, told me she loved me, and in one smooth movement ran the razorblade across her skin. Bright red blood poured out at the pace of her quickly beating heart. I couldn't believe she just did that. Maybe in the back of my mind I knew she brought me there to stop her, but how could I let this go on? She made a few more cuts and collapsed into the snow. I fell to my knees beside her, threw the razor away, and scrambled for my phone. She plead for me not to call, to let her die. I couldn't watch this anymore. I wrapped my shirt around her wrist and made the call.

And that was it. The penultimate nail in the coffin for her and I, whatever we were. She ended up in the psychiatric ward in one hospital, and I started my second admission to date in another. I spent New Year's Eve with patients who did not know what planet they were on, let alone what day it was. I remember they let us stay up and watch TV later than usual and even ordered a pizza for us. Once I got out, I received a registered letter from her and her parents asking for me to stay away from her. I hated myself for what I had done and punished myself every day with cutting and filling my body with drugs.

This continued for months and only worsened when I was charged for crimes I know in my heart I did not commit. In a 'He Said/She Said' legal system that would have cost me $35,000 to defend myself, I was forced to plead guilty. It was all the same to me at the time. I didn't give a fuck about my wellbeing. She made me believe I deserved to suffer; that I was a horrible person capable of the things she accused me of. I was truly broken, alone, and empty.

The next years were spent in a drug-fueled haze where my scars only multiplied and my self-loathing reached breaking points that lead to multiple suicide attempts and just as many hospitalizations. Relationships were an excuse to look for faults in my partner, the usual one being that they were not her. I still, for some reason, could not get the one who charged me out of my head, and I would be lying if I said I was truly free of her even today. Maybe it was the lack of closure.

If you read the first volume you can see my anger, hopelessness, drug addiction, and self-harm was quite apparent. I didn't hide anything. I was a monster and I showed it. I pushed anyone who cared away and alienated myself, only reinforcing the reason I did drugs in the first place. I was "happy" when I was numb. Nothing got to me and I could escape into a world where I was not some horrible monster, growing more grotesque by the day.

I guess the rest is history. I got better though, until I wasn't. Somehow I have fallen back into this pit of despair and I am seeing so much of my old self coming back, I am honestly scared that the monster I saw before never left, that it was only put in a cage and recently broke loose. That is what scares me. I am the same person capable of the same horrific acts and utter disregard for myself and those around me. I broke so many hearts, lost so much of myself and so many others, and most of all I have scars that remind me every day that even though the past is behind me, it is still inside me. Waiting? Scheming? Hungry?

So back to the original question: What is this all for? Fuck if I know. I may be better equipped and stronger than I was before, but is that enough? Can I win again? How much of myself will I lose in the battle? Who will I lose?

Fucking hell that was not easy to write. Shit.

- XV

Shakes and Aches
December 6th

It seems the shakiness and uneasiness is back. Maybe it's the Zoloft beginning to wreak havoc as it did six years ago. However, despite being on TWO antidepressants, I am still depressed. In my written journals from the first time I was given

Zoloft I talk about how it made me shaky, gave me insomnia, and made me "ramble". My thoughts raced relentlessly through my head, over and over again. I describe restless legs and increased anxiety around day 2 of treatment, and today is the third day and the same symptoms are appearing.

On day 3 (six years ago) I went nearly mad; cutting myself deeply on my arm at 3am and then wandering around town talking to myself, swearing that I was being followed. A snippet from the written journal goes as follows:

Nov 6 5:46am
"I feel paranoid and anxious now, like something terrible is about to happen. As I write this, my leg is shaking like Michael J. Fox on speed. This is not a good place for me. The doctor today is in for a treat. Oh yeah, and the gash on my arm is still bleeding. Hate life."

I really hope that these few days are not indicative of what is to come as it did last time. I am on a lower dose to start and will slowly increase, so there is a potential for the same effects to happen, but take longer to appear. I better be wrong, but knowing my luck as of late, I will probably be spot on in my prognosis.

- XV

Echo-cho-cho-cho-o-o
December 7th

I find my entries are starting to get repetitive. I'm sad and suffering, yeah – we've gathered that much. I truly wish I could sit here and write about happy things, good things, which do exist in my life, just not in the same proportion as the misery.

I am thankful for my amazing girlfriend (who is dealing with all of my mood swings pretty well), my supportive family and few friends, and my good (and stressful) job. I honestly do not have much else to be happy for. Every day seems to be the same old shit and I grow bored. Some part of my longs for the chaos of my past life. The thrill of the drugs, recklessness, and freedom to do nothing at all – they all call to me. It would be easy for me to slip back into that, but I just cannot bring myself to throw what I have away.

I'm fucking slipping into a void that seems harder to escape every day, and no one can give me any goddamn answers! The "Jon Snow" feeling (I know nothing…heh?) is the worst part of it. I'm being torn apart and I don't even know what the fuck is doing it. This faceless predator is eating away at my soul and no one can even give me an idea of what it is or why it is doing this. Just throw pills at the sad sack of shit! That ought to work just fine! Oops, wrong pill… Try this one. Shit, really? Hmm, this one?

And so on and so on. I barely slept last night and I feel like absolute garbage. I'm sluggish and melancholy. I feel like a zombie and sort of starting to look like one, too. I'm just done.

- XV

This Time In 2011…
December 7th

At this time, four years ago, my written journals speak of my world being shattered as yet another girl had left me due to my illness. I moped and wrote pages upon pages of how I fucked up and wasn't good enough and how I missed her. She had left in the night and I woke up to an empty bed and a text message.

I called myself "meaningless, unlovable trash" because she had ran away. I guess it took three years until I met my current girlfriend for me to feel good enough for someone again; to give myself a chance at being happy with someone, and in a healthy relationship. I am glad I did, though sometimes I still doubt myself as a person and as a partner.

The amount I obsessed over each failed relationship over those years was a testament to my loneliness and self-loathing. I found reason to push each one away and punish myself for losing them. Once they were gone, I would fall face first into a pile of cocaine or pills and numb out the feelings for as long as I could. Maybe that's why things are harder now – I don't numb like I used to.

The next year I was depressed over another ex of mine getting married. More self-loathing and hatred towards her for leaving me behind, even though she had every reason to do so, and more. I was freaking out over my anxiety, lack of sleep, and rising anxiety (much like now, I suppose). I feel like when I read these entries in my written journals, another person wrote them. In a way that is true, but that was still me... IS still me. That's what scares me. That can be me again.

- XV

There is a Man
December 8th

When I look at him, I see a regular man. He is about 5'11" with brown hair and blue eyes. But as I look closer, there are bags under his eyes and a forced smile upon his face. He looks exhausted and there is not much light in his eyes. A blue that colour should shine brighter – odd. He is slightly slouched, moving slowly, seemingly without purpose – only because he has to.

I watch him interact with people sometimes. That's just it though, he is acting. He hides behind a well formed and highly practised mask. I can see right through it because I know pain. He is miserable but he is forced to be happy and positive. Maybe that's why he is so tired? He also looks skinny, mostly noticeable by how is clothes fit – or don't fit. It is noticeable that he has altered his belt to make it smaller and his pants are looser than they are meant to be, as is his shirt. The somewhat gaunt face brings my theory together.

I can only infer, from what I see, that this is a man who is heavily burdened, and has been for a while. He has fought a battle for years, doing just enough to stay alive. The scars are apparent when he itches his forearm. I can also tell he used to be more; used to be proud of himself and his future. Rob a man of that and you take away part of his soul, one he can never regain. He is not complete. There is something fundamental missing from his being and his psyche that will not let him be happy.

There is a man, and he is not well. There is a man, well, more of an abstraction as time goes by, and he suffers. He may never get the help he needs, and I can see in his eyes that he has lost most of his hope that things will get better. He feels emptier each day, struggling to find a reason to fight. Only she and them comes to mind. Everything else is meaningless. Everything else will never be enough.

- XV

Keep the Anger Down
December 8th

It is getting more and more difficult to keep the irritability and anger down. The smallest things will set me off, and it especially shows at work. Right now I am temporarily in a management role, which with my anxiety, is tasking to say the least. I did this same role in the summer and though it was tough, I still rocked it. Now, I am a disorganized mess barely keeping my head above water.

One of the few things I pride myself in is my job and how I do at it. I love my job and it shows in the work I do. When I am unable to do the work to my standards, it bugs the fucking shit out of me.

Anyway, I guess this will be over next week so all I can do until then is get by the best I can.

- XV

I Am the Cursed
December 9th

Sometimes I wonder if I am cursed. From the start, all those years ago, it has been shit-storm after shit-storm. I do not take for granted the good in my life, but I cannot ignore the bad. By now you know what I am happy about and what I am not. It is so fucking hard to forget the past, even though mine feels like it was lived by someone else; a doppelganger who was intent on self-destruction and chaos.

The past will always be there, whether subtly in the background, huddled just outside of conscious thought or screaming in your face of your fuck-ups and failures. Mine is carved into my body just as much as it is into my psyche; a perpetual reminder that once I wanted to end it all, or at least make myself as ugly outside as I felt inside.

I am left, after all this, in the present, pouring my soul into a journal that may be meaningless in the end. As my hands hover over the keyboard, shaking from the seemingly idiopathic anxiety I feel, I wonder why my life turned out as it did. I may drive myself crazy thinking about it. Maybe there is no answer and fate (or circumstance) is just a huge fucking bitch sometimes.

Before, I chose to, and sometimes still, wallow in my misery. Before I would pop a pill, snort a line, and make a cut all the while lamenting the shitty hand I had been dealt. Now I write entry after entry trying to articulate my misery, hoping that by unloading my brain maybe I can understand what is going on. Maybe the real purpose of me publishing my first journals is so someone can tell me what is wrong with me. The professionals sure as shit can't.

Understand that this is for me. This journal. A place where I can empty my head, pour out my broken soul, and look back on myself with no judgements and no pressure to say the right thing. I write what comes to mind, with purpose, no omissions or censoring. I rarely hit backspace except to correct spelling because I truly believe whatever comes to mind first is the most truthful and raw. That is what this collection is.

- XV

Pulling Me Down
December 9th

I am not in a good place right now, even since my entry earlier today. Something is in my head and I can feel it in my heart. I don't know what exactly it is, but I can see foggy outlines of people and things I have seen before and the feeling in my chest is horrible. It's like a feeling of impending doom, except the doom has happened already. Echoes of the past resonate through my chaotic head, taunting – no, torturing me with things I should have left behind years ago.

Why does it still have this effect on me? Why do I hang onto these memories and let them tear me apart? It's like I am holding onto an anchor as it sinks into a bottomless pit, too stubborn or fucked up to let go. It seems masochistic to put myself through this, and maybe to some extent this is intentional. I could identify with being depressed and broken so much that I hold onto things that vindicate my identity.

How the fuck am I supposed to forget so much pain and heart-break? So many days, months, even years spent alone and fucked up because I couldn't stand the thought of what has been done to me, or what I have done to others. I am beginning to believe that this will never go away, that I am damned to live this way until I die. Sound dramatic? It probably is, but it's how I feel so suck it.

This "nostalgic virus" in my brain is tormenting me; playing sick games with my fragile psyche. I spoke before of being dealt a shitty hand, but maybe all that has led me here is circumstance, not fate. Maybe I could have pulled out of that nosedive six years ago without my illness getting this bad if that girl had not tried to kill herself, or I stopped her sooner. Maybe without the drugs the treatments would have worked and I could have healed long ago with minimal damage. Maybe If I wasn't so fucking self-absorbed in my own shit I would have listened to those who could help me.

Anyway, what fucking good does asking 'what ifs' do for me? Circumstance has led me to this place and it is up to me to make of it what I will, at least what is in my control. Whether I have BPD or bipolar or depression really makes no difference, in the long run. I am sick, I need the right treatment, and I need to let go. I just can't. For some reason I foolishly hang on as if it were my tether to sanity. The ironic part is it is only driving me insane, to the brink of something worse. The horizon looks foreboding, with blackness threatening to overtake the crimson hue that it is now.

- XV

Hostility
December 10th

My girlfriend and I had a rare fight-like thing tonight. We don't fight the way normal couples do – we get all quiet and passive aggressive. Anyway, things with us tend to build up and then explode at the most random of times. This is because she has trouble expressing herself or articulating her emotions, so when I do something stupid, it doesn't get dealt with until the aforementioned explosion.

To be completely honest, it bothers me that she cannot express herself, though I know it is through no fault of her own. Words just don't come easy for her and I can more than understand the anxiety it can cause. However, to be in a relationship communication is the key to survival. My point on this is how a relationship can last when the most basic things cannot be said? I have a great deal of anxiety over all the things she is potentially not telling me, whether I have reason to believe there is something or not. It's not always rational.

Of course, I blamed myself. I shut down and all I could think of was how can I be so stupid? I don't even realize that I get angry with her when she can't express herself, and it hurts her, which is understandable. She said me telling her to "just talk about it" would be like her saying to me, "just be happy". When she said that I realized that in fact there was a similarity there, one I had not thought of. Lately, she says I have just been not thinking. I would hate to be so caught up in my own issues that she gets pushed to the side.

She is the reason I still fight (however little) to maintain my sanity. I cannot lose her. I can't. I can't imagine what I would do to myself if I pushed her away and I was left alone again. Call me weak, but it is the cold, hard truth.

My mind is a fucking mess. Processing what was said tonight will not be easy, and I will take it to heart and beat myself up for it as I usually do. I am in for a rough night.

- XV

It's Happening Again
December 12th

Today I increased my Zoloft another 25mg to 75mg. The effects I felt six years ago did not take long to show themselves. If it weren't for this wonderful drug called Ativan, I could not be writing this right now. The shakes were the worst they have been in a long time, I was cold, nauseated, anxious, and my fast-moving jaw made my teeth chatter. It was not a pretty sight. My girlfriend is quite worried but I assured her if things got worse I would seek help.

I see my psychiatrist again in two days so hopefully either the effects will be gone by then or he will have another idea of what to try (like I need another medication to take). My counsellor is coming into the visit with me so hopefully she can pull more answers out of him than I have been able to. I am pretty sure he is working toward something, but it's the not knowing that is fucking with me.

Other than that, I feel shitty. I was up at that magic hour again, 5am, for absolutely no reason except my brain is a douchebag who likes to fuck with me. This lack of sleep is having a profound effect on my body and I can feel the first stages of a cold trying to sneak in. I'm so tired I can't even focus right now. As the Ativan wears off, so will my ability to continue writing, so I'll make this brief and pick up later.

Final thing is the trouble keeping track of my medications. I now take 3 Zoloft, 2 Wellbutrin, and 1 clonazepam in the morning, 1 Ativan if needed throughout the day, and at night I take 3 Divalproex, 2 clonazepam, 2 Abilify, and 1 trazodone. Let's do the math: that is 15 pills a day. FIFTEEN!!! Considering how I sign each entry it is also kind of cool, but I digress. Despite the EIGHT pills I take at night, I still cannot sleep. I can't fall asleep or stay asleep when I do happen to drift off.

I need to see something change soon or I am going to snap. I cannot take much more of this.

- XV

Zoloft Can Suck My Dick
December 13th

"When you have insomnia, you're never really asleep... and you're never really awake."
- The Narrator, Fight Club

Once again I have woken up at around 5:00am, tossing and turning as my girlfriend slept peacefully beside her. I'd be lying if I said I didn't resent her just a little. In a loving way of course. The shakes are bad still, however a pre-emptive dose of clonazepam seems to have lessened the severity of said shakes. My appetite is still low and I have dropped below 170lbs; a point where I said I would begin to worry if I dipped below it.

I feel restless and uneasy, with a slight feeling of impending doom spidering up from my heart every once in a while. The pain in my legs is getting unbearable. It feels like I have been running for days, and in a way I have. My legs are shaking the worst. Akathisia, my doctor calls it. Well good work, slick! You reduced one dose of a medication I am on to stop it and it worked for a bit, until you put me on another one that causes it!

Good thing tomorrow I see him, along with my counsellor. It should be a very interesting meeting with both of the professionals who are trying to figure me out talking, and most likely butting heads a little over my diagnosis and treatment plan. I will certainly update on how that goes after the appointment.

My girlfriend and I got in a few 'heated discussions' over the last few days about our future. With everything in my life so up in the air, I cannot realistically think long term. I know I want to be with her, more than anything, however I cannot think about where we will live, what I will be doing for school, or whatever else she asks me. To me, I just need to get through each day without losing my mind. Once I begin to feel better psychologically then the fog that disallows me to see my future will dissipate and I will gain some clarity.

For now, I am simply in survival mode.

- XV

Today's the Day
December 14th

My appointment with my doctor and counsellor is in one hour. To be completely honest, I am nervous about it. I feel like they have two very different views and may butt heads over my treatment. As you have previously read, my medication regiment is extreme, to say the least. He is carpet-bombing my body with pills and the effects are wearing me down.

I am unsteady, shaky, and anxious about my immediate future. What will come of this whole treatment "plan" of his? I know medications can only do so much, but I am also getting the treatment I need from my counsellor. Together, these treatments should be far more effective than I have seen.

In other news, I had a weird dream last night. It was really vivid and stuck with me. I was in a mental health treatment facility, except it looked more like a prison. This man was talking to me, holding a cross in one hand and a bible in the other. We were having a heated discussion about God. I remember him saying that it was all part of God's plan, and I needed to have faith. My response was, "Jesus Christ, if something goes right it's God's work, if something goes wrong it's part of God's plan! You guys have your asses covered. Fucked up? Apologize and the slate is wiped clean! I choose to live with my sins because they are part of who I am. I embrace my darker side!" As I was saying this, blackness started swirling around me and the man was being slowly disintegrated.

Then I woke up. At 5:00am, as per usual. My dreams are usually screwed up, but rarely stick with me this much. I am sure there is a lot of symbolism and whatever-the-fucks in there for people to tear apart into some kind of haphazard analysis (go ahead, analyze away!).

Anyway, I will post again after my appointment, hopefully in a good mood instead of a ranting, angry mood. Wish me luck.

- XV

Who Is the Doctor Here?
December 14th

The appointment went better than planned, but still had its moments. A good example is when I asked him how I could be on all these meds and not be getting better – I'm getting worse! Valid question right? Apparently not. He got all defensive and said, *"What do you think would happen if you went off all of these meds?"* To which I replied, "I don't know!" *"Well think about it!"* "I don't know! I must have missed that day in med school." *"You have a brain, think about it!"*

Turns out I would get worse, and that's not a good thing. See? I thought about that with my brain! He made me feel anxious for not knowing details on every one of my thoughts that race through my head while I attempt sleep, or how I couldn't articulate exactly what I am feeling, and of course, my lack of knowledge about pharmacology.

It really helped that my counsellor was there. I felt more comfortable and assured that at least someone will remember the medication changes and reminders he gave me. I'm foggy because I cannot sleep, an issue he refuses to address. Finally he agreed that some quetiapine would work well, but won't give it to me until the Abilify is out of my system. Tease. Guess I don't sleep until then, unless taking one less Abilify works somehow. I remain doubtful. The final medication change is that once I get off the Abilify, I can increase my Zoloft to 100mg!

I swore to him that Zoloft was causing me to be shaky and giving me restless legs. He assured me that it doesn't have that effect. Well my fucking ever-shaking legs and hands, which got worse after taking Zoloft would beg to differ. I'll just go fuck myself. Really. Write out the prescription for the meds and I will take them if it means I don't have to listen to your condescending banter anymore.

Guess the ranting, angry mood won!

- XV

Tenebris
December 15th

Something wicked this way comes, sinister and bearing its teeth in hateful disgust. He has had so much taken from him that revenge is all that shines in his black eyes. He has lived in pain, taken beating after savage beating, and now he is ready to fight back against an insidious and shapeless entity that has plagued him for too long.

It is time he took control of his own life and no longer let the marionette strings guide him down a path of darkness and regret.

There is simply too much on the line to give up and give in. He has nearly lost his life too many times to remember; lost too much of himself to ever be complete again. Harlots with innocent eyes and smiles beckoning him, pulling him in only to destroy him. For years he mused over them, unable to let go despite what they did. Still, to this day, they occupy space in his mind and sometimes step forward to remind him of Hell.

So now he stands at a crossroads. One path presumably leading to happiness and the other (presumably) to pain. The thing about presumptions is that they often assume that the world works in simple ways; that life is always option A or B. The reality is there are infinite possibilities for outcomes based on your actions, and predicting them is near impossible. He chooses the path of happiness, but he is ignorant to what is along the way. Obstacles he never dreamed of, pain he never thought possible, and situations so hopeless the allegory of falling into an abyss doesn't come close to equating how forlorn the possibility of escape is.

He stumbles along the path, and though he is aware that the path is long and treacherous, at the end lies happiness and that is worth fighting for. So he takes the meds, climbs the obstacles, and fights on. Doubts arise. Who said that happiness is even possible for him? Who said this is the path that leads there? Who says he will survive to get to the end even if it exists?

Optimism can only get you so far. Realism and pessimism sometimes fall together perfectly. Is being positive and ignorant better than being realistic and aware that shit happens? We all love to be warm and fuzzy, pretending everything is okay and all wounds can be healed. The truth is some people are too fucking far gone to be saved. That may not be the case for this man, but he may be damned to a life of walking this path but never reaching the end, as with Sisyphus and the boulder.

This man has an abnormal normal, where his baseline is shit, his low points shittier, and his high points barely begin to emulate happiness. He would much rather be aware that this is a life-long fight, and nothing is guaranteed when fighting such a faceless and evil slut as mental illness. The brain turned against itself is a powerful thing, capable of things so horrific that we pop pills, cut ourselves, or commit suicide to avoid them. It is NOT weakness. It, for them, is the only escape from a life that has become too much to bear. Understand people, people. Stop judging and start learning.

- XV

Good Morning, World!
December 16th

It is currently 5:22am and I have been up for an hour. I even walked down to Tim Horton's and got a coffee. I knew as soon as I woke up that there was no chance of getting any more sleep. You get to know these feelings the longer sleep eludes you. Waking up in a foggy haze oddly enough brings about a certain clarity that allows you to understand yourself better. My body simply cannot, or doesn't want to, sleep.

I am slowly wasting away. I have lost 17 pounds since October 27th. Yes, SEVENTEEN. I am almost six feet tall and weigh around 166lbs. I feel like the barrier I have built that keeps all the bad things at bay is slowly crumbling with each shitty sleep, each missed meal, and each handful of pills. This is not natural. I don't even want to think about what all of these pills and a shitty diet is doing to my body. The doctor seems to think all is well, so who am I to argue? *The patient. Who feels the pain, every day?* Good point.

I'm just lost. I am so far off the map I cannot even see it anymore. It feels like I have been stumbling for six years between doctors and meds and drugs and fix-me-therapies, but just keep enough balance not to fall on my face and never get up again. I used to long for chaos, week-long drug benders, meaningless hook-ups, and solitude. Though I have come this far, those parts of my life are not necessarily 100% behind me.

When I am at my worst, these feelings creep out from the shadows and threaten to take hold of me as they did for all those years. The only reason I don't give in is because now I have too much to lose. I have come too far to fall back into a pile of coke, a sea of pills, or a pool of my own blood. The poison inside of me will never be completely gone, all I can do is deal with it as it bears its ugly fucking face.

- XV

Conundrum
December 16th

Doctors have been scrambling to diagnose me for years, to put me in this neat little box so they can understand and treat. Labels are necessary, right? In my case, a solid diagnosis is nothing but a dream at this point. I have always been described as 'borderline' mostly because I didn't really fit in anywhere. The copious amount of drugs I did certainly did not help them gain any clarity. What was psychopathological and what was drug-induced?

Still I search for an answer to what I have. I do not know why I need the label so much. It may be that the mystery, the not knowing, is what really bothers me. I am the type of person who needs to know what something is, be able to define it, and ultimately understand it. So what is the answer?

I have named these volumes after a mental illness that was laid on me several times in the past. It fit me almost perfectly and with that label, I could put a name to the invisible ball of shit that was ruining my life. I could research it, talk to other people who had it, and be treated for it. Clearly the treatment was ineffective as you may have noticed by now.

Enter my new psychiatrist who, after asking me a slew of questions, gave me a new label – bipolar II disorder. Fuck. What now? I have had to reassess everything I had thought about myself and what has tormented me for all these years. I guess it was a sort of existential crisis in that I let BPD define me in some ways. It was my answer, my excuse for everything, and the only thing even close to certainty I had until recently.

My psychiatrist is having a hard time selling bipolar to me. His biggest reason behind it is that I have far too many physical symptoms for this to be a personality disorder. Fair, I can see his point. Secondly, my mania is more hypomania, characteristic of bipolar II. Next, it runs in my family. My paternal uncle has it as well and has not had an easy life because of it. Lastly, he simply said that the previous treatment did not work.

It seems he is working hard to make the diagnosis stick, almost to the point of asking questions and hoping to hear a certain answer (remember before when I said there seemed like a right and wrong answer to his questions?). He is confused by my hypomania due to the fact that although I am restless, anxious, and irritable, I am too sluggish (representative of a depressive state). Usually people with mania move from one thing to another quickly and in a disorganized way – which I don't.

He continues to study the conundrum that is myself and I give him bonus points for sticking with it. My identity crisis is secondary to that. I need to give the meds time to work and him time to find the right balance.

I will NOT, however, change the title of this book or the first!

- XV

Out of Hand
December 17th

This fucking bullshit is too much. I am so close to being done with it. I can't even keep food down anymore, I'm weak and frail, losing my mind, and I feel like I am on auto-pilot. I passed my wit's end about a hundred miles ago. I am resenting my own body and mind for not being 'normal' and not responding to the plethora of drugs that I am taking every day.

I rarely admit that things are bad or when I am in a lot of pain. I usually go the quiet route (at least outside of this journal) and keep it to myself, suffering in silence. It is getting harder and harder to keep that silence. I want to scream that I am not okay, that I am in physical and psychological pain, and that I cannot take much more of it before I finally snap. I try, but words escape me when I try to talk to people about it. I have told my girlfriend, counsellor, and a good friend that my condition has not been this bad in years, but articulating it into a way that makes sense is an impossible feat.

How can I possibly put into words something that even I cannot understand? Something so fucking abstract and intangible that all the world's shrinks and all the world's experts cannot figure it out. I feel like I am repeating myself lately with entries talking about my pain and confusion, my condition and hopelessness, and my desperation and resentment. I honestly don't know how else to say it. This is something I am still trying to figure out. Maybe writing dozens of entries will give me some insight into what the fuck is going on (though I doubt it).

Tomorrow I increase my Zoloft and hopefully get a prescription for something to help me sleep (maybe quetiapine). Sleep is the first thing I need to get under control before addressing all of my other issues. I don't care if I don't eat for days or puke every time I do eat, I just want some fucking decent sleep!

- XV

Metaphor?
December 18th

I had a dream last night. Lucid and frightening.

The ground is cracking and caving in underneath me. The earth shudders with each hit I take. I try to keep balance, instead I stumble down a blind path hoping for even ground ahead. The fog is too thick to see anything at all. It feels like I am being stung by a hundred bees, but I cannot see anything on my skin. My head is pounding and my stomach is cramped. Desperately I reach out for something to hold onto, something to give me an idea of where I am. Instead, my hand burns as if acid was poured on them, so I recoil it in terror. What is happening? Where am I? Can I escape? A cascade of questions flow through my mind as visions appear and disappear in the peripherals of my vision. The ground quakes harder and I am now crawling along on my hands and knees, nearly being pulled into the yawning voids that appear underneath me. The fog clears up, but only slightly. I begin to see silhouettes in the distance and somehow they are familiar to me. They surround me on all sides bearing down on me and keeping their balance despite the violent shaking. I recognize some of the figures as they get close to me. Her? And Her? Him? Excruciating pain tears through my body as I watch all my old scars split open and pour crimson blood onto the ground. Gasping for air I finally fall to the ground. I lay on my back looking up at a purple sky. Pills begin to fall like rain around me, all different shapes, sizes, and colours. The pool of blood spreads and starts seeping into the cracks as I grow weak. The figures are now directly over me, their arms combining to choke me out as I lay helpless on the ground. Relief washes over me as I gasp out my final breath. It was over.

Yep. What the fuck, right? It seems to be a pretty clear metaphor for how my life is going right now, but it is the end that scares me the most.

- XV

Autopilot
December 19th

Yesterday was a rough one. It seems that dream I had set the tone for what would become a very strange and surreal day. From the time I awoke I felt that something was just off. I cannot explain it, but it just seemed like I was floating through the day like a plastic bag in the wind. The shakes were pretty bad too, making it hard to even type at work. It felt like I was on autopilot, but somehow maintained enough control to stumble through the day until I could get home.

My mood was different too. I had noticeably less affect than usual and I was sluggish and not making jokes as much as I usually do. My girlfriend knew when she came over that something was off, and even as I tried to explain it, she began to worry about what was going on in my body. She did some research and saw that I had symptoms of sleep deprivation, medication withdrawal, and even overdose. I am going to put my money on the former being the case, here.

All I knew was that there was something wrong with the Force that day. It only got worse as the night went on, culminating in me once gain throwing up my dinner (a delicious Swiss Chalet festive special, I might add). I was so weak she needed to help me up and get me to my bed. Everything hurt and I wanted to scream in frustration and anger. If it wasn't for her to keep me from doing shit like that, I don't know how things would be for me.

Night one of the Seroquel the doctor gave me for sleep was a complete and utter failure, with me once again waking up in the wee hours of the morning to toss and turn in bed and trying not to wake my girlfriend up as the restlessness became worse and worse. I had high hopes for this medication to finally get me a full night's sleep, but maybe tonight will be better. Why do I have to be so immune to things that would otherwise knock someone else out for 16 hours?

SO now I sit here, typing away as the shakes get worse. They always do this time of day, as does my mood drop. More recently my mood has just been simply disappearing. What the fuck am I supposed to do? I am so lost.

- XV

Dehumanized
December 20th

The life is being drained from me as if there is a slow leak I cannot see. Each day brings more exhaustion, flatter affect, and more depression and hopelessness. I barely feel human anymore, to be honest. I am so fucking good at going through the motions that I tricked even myself. I wore a mask even I was blind to, until it began cracking and falling apart. Slowly I would see a side of me I had not laid eyes on in quite a while, then it would be gone.

Now it is mostly there, visible beneath the surface. The toxic effects were clear in my strained relationship. Don't get me wrong, she and I are okay, but she is as lost as I am about what to do. I think she is more worried than she is letting on, as well. Anyway I just feel like the human part of me is being sapped out by this malevolent force and being replaced with nothing at all. I still cannot get a decent sleep despite adding the Seroquel on top of everything else, and I know that it is taking a huge toll on my body. Every time I look into the mirror I see more entity than man, more hollow than the time before.

If this continues I will lose myself completely. People keep telling me this is temporary and things will get better. I am fucking tired of hearing that because things can go to shit just as easily. Once again we have a classic case of pessimism vs realism. How can I just focus on the potential good when the current bad is mushroom-slapping me in the face? I am so surrounded by shit that I can't even look too far into the future, even if I wanted to. I have to focus on the now, what is hurting me the most and go from there. It's like patching up a dam but leaks keep springing up as you fix the previous one.

I bought a Fitbit today, something that tracks my steps and sleep. This was requested by my psychiatrist so he can gauge my restlessness and erratic sleep patterns. It will be interesting to see what results I get from the sleep tracker tonight. I am not optimistic.

- XV

The Most Wonderful Time of the Year
December 21st

Apparently it is supposed to be wonderful, but for me it historically hasn't been. I hate the very idea of a holiday that has become so much about consumerism that we have lost ourselves in blow-out sales and spending money on stupid shit we don't even need. I can't even imagine the money people put out for this fucking holiday (which in itself is flawed in nature due to the historical inaccuracies of the reason we celebrate this time of year), putting themselves in debt so little Timmy can have his X-Box.

On top of that, the stress of gift buying is enormous, as is that of figuring out where you are going to spend Christmas. Being a child of divorce means two or more Christmases where you go back and forth and fall even farther away from the intended meaning of the holiday. My idea of a good Christmas is spending time with those you love, maybe indulging in some nice, strong eggnog, maybe play a board game, and exchange a few cheap gifts. Alas, that is not how shit is anymore.

That rant aside, this time of year usually digs up old memories such as this being the time that changed my life forever when she tried to kill herself in that forest, forcing me to spend New Year's in the psych ward. Let's not go there.

Of course this is a time where people reflect on what they have done over the year, either making them proud or miserable or both. I have very mixed feelings about this year, and I will shockingly focus on the good first. My girlfriend and I have only grown closer and more certain that we want a future together. I love every second I am with her and she has done so much to keep me from slipping over the edge. My job has been good to me, and I now have a permanent position for as long as I'd like (not forever, hopefully). Things are good with my family and my few friends as well.

Now for the negative. My depression and anxiety and whatever-the-fuck else has once again reared its ugly head. Something I had thought was behind me is back, and this time it's different. I was in a university program I enjoyed then was booted because of my bullshit criminal record. That was the beginning of a long, slow slide back down into the shit and the piss. I have been fighting it again ever since. Now there is a new diagnosis of bipolar II disorder and I feel like my identity has been destroyed, like I don't know who I am anymore.

I honestly do not know what to think about the year 2015. It has held both pleasant surprises and horrible times, and truly tested the limits of my psyche. I cannot even think about 2016 when there is such a shit storm surrounding me, but hopefully it is a year of improvement and healing.

- XV

Holding Onto the Past
December 22nd

I said we weren't going to go there, but six years ago today my girlfriend at the time (or whatever she was to me) attempted suicide. Surely by now the basic details regarding what happened are obvious. I cannot remember what I have already said in previous entries, but the events culminated in her attempted suicide by overdose and slit wrists – while I was right beside her. My guilt over what happened was immediate, only compounded by accusations from her family and mine. How could I stand by and watch someone I love do this?

You simply cannot know unless you were there. I was trapped. All roads seemed to lead to her death, so why should she do it alone? Maybe I was rationalizing an act that I hated myself for being a part of. The guilt ate me alive as I scarred my body inside and out, punishing myself over and over. I guess today I still feel some of that guilt. It is not a night you just forget and move on from. I don't think the guilt will ever be completely gone, but each year it gets a little easier.

I wonder if this day bothers her as much, or if it is just another square on the calendar to her. Why do I even care? Why can't I let go? My mind wanders to her and the damage she has done when I am mentally weakest. I believe the problem is I never got closure. One moment she was there and things were good, and the next I was in a jail cell wondering what the fuck had just happened.

My counsellor asked me today what would help me let go, and of course I said closure. She asked what I wanted to hear and all I said was I wanted her to tell me she placed that letter there and that she forgives me. Six years is a long time to be fucked up over someone who tore your heart out and pissed on it, but it seems things are much more complicated than simply moving on. I honestly don't know what I would say, or what her to say for that matter.

I feel weak and insane for even bringing this up, hell, for even having these memories surface. She is like fucking herpes, always there but flares up from time to time. On the bright side I see a friend today who I haven't seen in a while. It will be really nice to see her again and go grab some sushi.

- XV

Choking On the Cloud
December 23rd

This is supposed to be a happy fucking time of year, but instead the clouds are only darkening and thickening, choking me out. I feel this heavy weight upon me that is getting heavier each day. I know that my lack of sleep has a lot to do with this. According to my Fitbit, I slept 3 hours and 52 minutes last night, 4 hours and 34 minutes the night before, and 5 hours and 24 minutes the night before that.

I am in a permanent fog now and everything seems unreal. It is the same kind of dissociative feeling as before, but worse. I am having trouble doing something as simple as typing this entry, and thoughts are not coming to me as easily as they usually do. I am unfocused, unaware, and I know that I am on the verge of a mental breakdown. I can't do this anymore. I just fucking can't.

- XV

Fucking Christmas Eve
December 24th

Well it is Christmas Eve and I am alone in my room. I do have family upstairs, but I am not myself. I feel hate and anger and resentment mixed together, but no one has done anything to make me feel that way. I don't feel right and I think it is better off if I am alone for the time being.

My doctor upped my Seroquel dose to 200mg from 50mg, so I better fucking sleep tonight. If I don't, this problem goes much deeper than what medication can fix. I have never been so drained, so exhausted, so fucking done with everything that all I want to do is lay down in peace and forget everything. I want no human interaction, no expectations – I simply want time to myself. I know that will never happen and it pisses me off.

In this time of joy and good will towards men (and women), I feel nothing. No joy, no happiness, no excitement for Christmas or the new year, and no comfort. Fuck this entry. I am done.

- XV

Black and White Christmas
December 25th

I feel nothing. It is as if something has sucked all the emotion out of me and left me an empty shell. No happiness, no sadness, no anger, no joy – nothing. I feel as flat as a sheet of paper. This is the inevitable time where the emptiness takes over and I become a zombie. The Seroquel sure isn't helping with that feeling either.

It all sounds so cliché, me saying that the world appears black and white, drained of all colour. That I have been sapped of all feelings and left with nothing but a few sparse remains of who I was. I have no drive to write, get out of bed, take care of myself, eat, or anything else. I would be worried if I could feel that way.

- XV

Hollowed Out
December 28th

"If there's a bright side to this suffering
Can you help me see?
It's getting harder to believe

You always said that this would not last long
But it's gone on and on and on
And I just can't make it stop

Hey, is your heart still beating?
I can't stop the bleeding
I've lost you completely

Hey, gather all the heartache
I'll hold it in my hand
Just to lose it all again

They're right this time
I won't pretend to smile
Because inside,
I'm black and I'm hollow"

- The Bright Side of Suffering – Scary Kids   Scaring Kids

As you may have noticed, things have not improved in the few days since my last post. I continue to feel the life draining from my veins. I was out seeing family this weekend and it was a constant battle to look like I was there, not drifting off into nothingness. I was caught a few times with my head in the clouds and brushed it off as me simply being tired. Truth is, I just don't fucking care anymore. I am so done and so empty that nothing interests me.

I don't know whether it is the medication or my condition doing this to me, but it is not heading in a good direction. I slip more each and every day into a state of semi-consciousness. Every task seems daunting and typing this is so fucking hard I may just forget these entries all together.

I am failing to see a bright side anymore, failing to see a silver-lining where I can at least say that this is all for something. There is no meaning, no reason, and no end in sight. I am fucking sick of pretending.

- XV

Countdown
December 29th

This will likely be my last post before the New Year, unless I think of something later tonight. I am spending New Year's in Toronto with my girlfriend and leave tomorrow for her place.

There is little need to do a big review and an in-depth analysis of the year that just passed. Surely by now the ups and downs and my feeling about both are well-known. It was a year that started well and took a horrible turn as I began losing what I had fought so hard to gain. Without the support of my family and amazing girlfriend, I would surely have reverted back to old habits and lost even more of myself.

Fighting for my sanity and my life has been hard, and I know that this coming year will be a continuation of a war that began over six years ago. Looking back, I am honestly amazed at the very fact that I am still alive. My utter disregard for my health, both mental and physical, nearly destroyed me. Through multiple hospitalizations, overdoses, countless stitches, endless nights alone in misery, and one drug after another I somehow survived. In my eyes, parts of me died with each attempt to end my life. Other parts of me were taken with each person I gave my heart to before I watched them run away.

The voids left inside will remain with me forever, forcing me to rebuild a life around mangled holes and shattered pieces. Though tattered and torn I push forward against the weight of a thousand horrific memories toward an ideal 'me', whatever the fuck that is. I constantly feel the aftermath of my previous life, unable to let go of people and things that only serve to remind me of the worst times of my life. Maybe they will haunt me forever, or maybe one day I will be able to let go. For now I bear all of it upon my shoulders and in my weakened heart.

I never make resolutions for the New Year. I do not need some empty promise made with no accountability to guide me where I need to go. I simply take my life one day at a time, hoping to keep my head above water until I can figure out my purpose here, or even better, who the fuck I am. Maybe 2016 will bring about change for the good. Maybe it will be the year I finally face and defeat my demons, enabling me to move forward without the weight of regret on me. Or things can continue to decline. I guess we will see.

Happy New Year

- XV

The Poison
December 29th

I guess one more post for the year is acceptable. I feel like I am straining my relationship with all the shit going on in my life.

She tries so hard to help and understand and I just seem to make her feel worse for it. I told myself I would never bring her down, and if it gets to the point where I feel like I am, I know I would run. Run before she can be poisoned by me as those who have had relationships with me in the past have.

I know she is different than them, and I am different than I was then, but there is still a huge part of me that can see the potential for destruction and focuses on that. I would sooner be admitted back to the psych ward indefinitely before doing any damage to her. I know better, but that doesn't mean it can't happen.

Losing her is simply out of the question.

- XV

When Monologue Becomes Dialogue
January 2nd, 2016

Well, here it is – 2016, a year of possibilities. I don't know what I expect from this year, but making resolutions and making a big deal over a number in the date changing isn't like me.

We all have that ever-present inner monologue in our heads. A voice that guides us through the day, from spotting dangers to making decisions. It is there in everyone. Lately, my inner monologue has become more of a dialogue, where questions I ask myself seem to be answered by someone else inside of my head. Sometimes I recognize the person, and sometimes it seems to be talking to a different version of myself.

I don't know if I should be worried about this or if it is just my process. However, this is new and causes me a great deal of anxiety when it occurs. It is sort of like the devil on my shoulder, except more and more often it is taking the form of someone from my past. She taunts and jokes from inside my head, appearing at random to torment me and point out everything that is fucked up in my life.

Maybe I will go look this up before saying any more about it; I do not want to jump the gun on something with potentially damaging consequences. I just don't understand what is going on in my head, and that's what scares me.

- XV

R.I.P. Grandpa
January 5th

This morning I lost my grandpa. He died in his sleep after several years of battling ALS and cancer. When I was only five years old, the doctors gave him only a few years to live. Twenty years later, it was finally too much for him. When I saw him over Christmas I knew he did not look himself, but I never would have guessed only a few weeks later he would take his last breath. At least he went peacefully in his sleep.

My grandpa was not only the toughest man I knew, but the funniest and warmest. He had a joke for everything and his love for his family was immense. During his years in the military he was well-respected and rose through the ranks quickly. His dedication to our family was steadfast.

I don't think the reality has set in for me yet. It will take time to believe this is real, and although I know his suffering is over, I will miss him with all my heart.

- XV

Mourning
January 7th

The last few days have been weird for me. The reality that I have lost my grandpa has not set in yet. As my girlfriend said, nothing has really changed for me as of yet. I have not had to face the fact he is really gone. That will not be until the funeral on Saturday. I feel like I have been in a haze, where everything seems surreal, as if soon I will wake up and continue on with 'real life'.

She has really been amazing, spending the last few days with me as I begin to deal with my loss. Even more amazing is that she is not taking my rapid mood swings and irritated outbursts personally (at least she doesn't seem to be). I cannot really explain how I feel, and I doubt I will be able to until after the funeral. Until then I sit on the fringe, preparing to face what lies ahead.

- XV

Losing Grip
January 11th

Since I heard that my grandpa had passed on my days seem blurred together, separated only by an all too brief sleep. At the funeral he looked good, almost 20 years younger. As soon as I saw him the floodgates opened and I cried for the first time in as long as I can remember. I was a mess for a while, sobbing in the room outside where my grandpa lay. Slowly the numbness came crawling back. As we left the funeral home and I took my last look at my grandpa, a switch flipped and again I was flat.

I drank that night until it didn't hurt so badly. Emotions were running high and it was chaos around me as a dozen conversations melded together into what sounded like white noise. I heard nothing specific, only a drone as I stared into my cup. I must have seemed thoughtful at the time but the truth is my brain was empty, as was my chest. I wanted to just slide into nothingness and disappear. Instead I continued drinking.

It surely does not help that my doctor increased my Seroquel again, taking away what little affect I had left. He also took me off my anti-depressant and restarted me on one he had taken me off. I cannot fucking keep track anymore. It is so fucking frustrating trying to explain how I feel to him when his mind is already made up about my mental state. Stubborn asshole.

When I do sleep my dreams are lucid and make no sense. In one, I stood in the middle of a dark, musty room. The sound of steadily dripping water came from one of the walls. I went closer and realized it was blood, not water. As I touched it, my hand stuck to the wall and I was slowly being pulled in. When I came out on the other side I was greeted by flames as high as radio towers and heat so excruciating I would double over in pain. There's a voice that comes up over the roar of the fire, and all it says is "break". I'm no Sigmund Freud so I will not even try to delve into my mind and decipher these dreams. They could be as pointless as nipples on a man, or they could be of vital importance into my state of mind. Who the hell knows? I just feel like I am losing grip on reality.

Today was my first day back at work. I don't feel ready but I cannot afford to take the time off. I kept mostly to myself, doing menial and repetitive work until it was time to go home. I am hoping for a snow day tomorrow but it does not seem very likely. Fuck.

- XV

Culmination (Epilogue)
January 12th

I have been journaling in some form or another since November of 2009, when my symptoms first appeared. I don't know why I started, but it did enable me to get things out of my head that were bothering me and put in on paper. I guess I hoped to make some sense of what seemed senseless to me at the time. I was okay and on a path that I was confident in. Going into second year at Queen's was huge for me and I was passionate about my choice in psychology as a major. Until I wasn't.

It seemed like overnight my drive was taken from me. All motivation and forward momentum was sapped from my body and I was left empty. I spent so much time sleeping that I barely had a life. It wasn't until my roommates told me I had a problem that I looked for help. I was wasting away and I had no idea why. This was the beginning of a six year (and counting) story that would bring highs and lows like no other. It is safe to say that with my self-injurious acts, I have barely survived this horrible mental illness, whatever it may be.

Bipolar, borderline, depressed, manic, or all of the above – it doesn't matter to me anymore. To be completely candid, I have lost any motivation to put a label on what it is I have. As for the treatment, I have given up trying to understand it. Every time I see my doctor now I am left with a prescription where he has started or stopped a medication, upped the dose or lowered the dose. Besides keeping my pharmacist on her toes it has shown me that he simply cannot get it right. He seems to be putting out fires as they pop up instead of understanding and treating the reason the fires start in the first place.

By now it is crystal clear that I pour my heart into these pages, looking for some kind of resolution, some catharsis, or even just some fucking insight into what exactly is going on in my head. If my life were a scatter plot of ups and downs, one would find no correlation, just the outline of a massive question mark among the chaos. What I hope would come from all of this work has not came, and probably never will. Maybe this is my way of putting out the fires in my head – journal and hope that it empties out some of the flammable material. All I do know is that the therapeutic value of journaling has dwindled for me. As I feel myself slipping away, it becomes harder to focus or attach myself to anything.

I am not sure if it is the cocktail of medications I am on or an evolution of my psychopathology, but I feel distant, flat, and empty. The highs don't feel so high and the lows are not so pronounced. Keep in mind though, my 'norm' is low to begin with, so when I say I am low I really mean it. I just feel like a fucking ghost sometimes. Other times like a robot, void of emotion and programmed to carry out the same routine day after day. Nothing excites me anymore, I look forward to nothing, I don't have the sense of humor I used to, and people are noticing that I do not look well. Mostly because my eyes are sunken into a pale visage that shows no emotion. I'm certain my behaviour is also a pretty big clue. It is getting harder to feign happiness for the benefit of others (something I have prided myself in being able to do, until now).

So what does all of this mean for me? Well, for starters it means that I am not okay. I am losing myself more and more, and it seems like there is nothing I can do. It also means my medication regimen will continue to turn me into a mindless drone, surely with implications on my social life and relationship. It may also compel me to take a break from journaling, as much as I would like to continue. The implications of a continued downward spiral are countless, and I will face each one the best I can with what I have. My worry is that soon I will not have the will or the strength to stand off against them. Surely that would end in me falling back to old habits that were nothing but self-destructive in nature.

I guess this is a wrap. I do not know what my future holds, so I will take it day by day. I hope this journal has helped me or eventually someone else understand an entity as elusive as mental illness. With any luck this journal will mean something to someone and become more than a place to empty my head into. But who knows? Maybe this was all for nothing.

- XV

THE END

Falter
July 27th, 2016

I am walking down a road, one that bifurcates often into endless possibilities. Each turn I take has consequence, an effect on my life that could be positive or detrimental. The road is uneven and I struggle to keep my footing as I walk in near darkness. Sometimes I carefully choose which path to take: right or left. Other times, I throw myself down a random road and hope for the best. Call it bad luck, shitty karma, or whatever-the-fuck, fact is, I usually choose wrong.

I think back at the path I have taken to get me where I am, especially the path that led me to her. I have said before that if all the pain, addictions, hospitalizations, and suicide attempts brought me to her, then it was worth it. I would do it all again for her, for an eternity if that is what it took. Walking the road with her was easier, lighter, and the decisions were made together. At some point I started faltering from the path and the separation became more and more profound. Then she took a right, I fell to the left and that was it. It was over. I lost the person I loved the most.

Before her I believed that happiness and stability was unobtainable for me, as evidenced by my sordid past. When I met her that changed. The pessimist in me was (nearly) quieted and pushed down as the optimist finally was able to come up for air. Part of me always knew I would blow it, but a bigger part of me knew that she was the one, the one I would do anything for. Actions speak louder than words I suppose. My own turmoil made me self-centred and she fell into the background of my misery. She didn't deserve that. She never did. I have to live with this monumental loss; the wrong turn that broke us up and brought the pessimist back.

- XV

Self-Discovery vs. Self-Destruction
November 10th

I find myself at a very interesting point in my life. I imagine it like being caught in zero gravity where everything floats around you, suspended in an entrancing ballet. Shards of who you were float amongst twisted metallic pieces of how you see yourself now. Televisions with only static on the screen show how you see the future as arrows made of expectations and harsh realities cause you to try to float away. I am waiting for the moment gravity is reintroduced and everything falls, leaving me a torn up mess. If I've learned anything over the past years, it is that gravity will always come back. The circle of life, I guess.

However as these grisly images go through my mind, so does a shocking revelation. It's shocking for me at least because it seems so fucking obvious and the fact that it took me this long to see it is an indictment of my intellect, quite frankly. It goes like this: I have attempted suicide over half a dozen times. Hospitalized myself to varying degrees as I trudged down my path of self-destruction. But what if they weren't suicide attempts? Stay with me now, we will get through this. Now if not suicide attempts, then what the fuck were they? The leading contenders if you randomly polled a group of people would almost certainly be "cry for help", "likes the pain and/or attention", or "too dumb to do it right". Now, despite the accusations of my intellect stated above, I know that option three is just plain wrong. Any idiot can easily off themselves, it's not all that hard. The other two? Just... no.

So then what the shit? Well to put it simply, it was a destructive mix of self-punishment and suicide. Wait, didn't I just say it wasn't suicide? Fuck this is confusing. Let me explain some more, random questions interrupting my entry. I never wanted to kill myself. I wanted to kill parts of myself. I saw the ugliness, the monsters with gnarled teeth and eyes black as coal and I wanted them dead. Poisoning myself to the point of near death would hopefully do the job, so I overdosed. Not that simple, apparently. Slicing the shit out of my arms? Maybe losing all of that blood would kill the nasty fucker. Not so much. All I ended up doing was smashing myself into bits and trying to fit them back together. Now all I have left are pieces laid in place separated by large cracks and weak mortar.

I find it so fucking hard to find motivation for anything now. I fail to see the point of doing my course because I simply do not want to. Fuck it. Fuck it all. Work is tedious but wonderfully repetitious. It's something I just go and do during the week before doing sweet fuck all on the weekends. I feel like the energy is being drained from me. I feel like any time I try to look to the future I see what everyone else wants for me and I panic. It feels like shit. But I cannot say anything. I just can't. I hate letting people down and there have been so many times where I have been a people pleaser at my own expense, only ending up miserable. It sounds like something a good person would do, I mean making people happy is good right? Not when you are doing shit you do not want to do. I feel hopeless because as it stands right now, all roads lead to loss. To pain. Maybe I am happy where I am! Maybe I like drinking, and the odd drug, and just trying to make the most out of the shitty fucking cards I have been dealt.

I have a lot to think about and my mind is hell. Which is pretty obvious by this entry. Fucking existential crises.

- XV

Connect With Topher Edwards On:

Facebook:
www.facebook.com/topheredwardsauthor

www.facebook.com/thebpdjournals

YouTube Channel:
Topher Edwards

Other Mental Health Resources:

Suicide Crisis Centres

Canada - www.suicideprevention.ca

United Kingdom - www.supportline.org.uk/

United States - www.suicidepreventionhotline.org

Australia - www.lifeline.org.au

Learn More About Mental Health and Mental Illness

Canadian Mental Health Association
http://www.cmha.ca/mental-health/understanding-mental-illness/

National Institute of Mental Health
www.nimh.nih.gov

If you or someone you know is having issues with mental health, please use the mental health services in your area. There are <u>always</u> ways to get help, and to help those around you. Be kind, listen without judgment, and do not perpetuate the stereotypes that feed the stigma. Having a safe, open space could save a life. If you feel alone in this fight, you are not. It takes time and courage, but you CAN reach out and someone will be there to listen.

Never stop fighting - mental illness won't.

- XV

CPSIA information can be obtained
at www.ICGtesting.com
Printed in the USA
LVOW13s0601070717
540445LV00003B/8/P